JAPANESE NOW

JAPANESE NOW

Teacher's Manual

Volume 4

ESTHER M. T. SATO
and
MASAKO SAKIHARA

University of Hawaii Press
Honolulu

MANUFACTURED IN THE UNITED STATES OF AMERICA
95 94 93 92 91 90 5 4 3 2 1

ISBN 0-8248-1248-4

PUBLICATION OF THIS BOOK HAS BEEN ASSISTED
BY A GRANT FROM THE JAPAN FOUNDATION.

CONTENTS

PREFACE

Volume 4 of *Japanese Now* is basically a reader introducing the student to both ancient and modern Japan. It consists of seventeen lessons that present a brief history of Japan through events that have characterized each of its major historical periods. These include political, social, and economic changes that have ultimately shaped the Japan of today.

Volumes 1 and 2 emphasized the development of listening and speaking skills, while Volume 3 gave priority to skills in reading at the same time that it provided more opportunity for practice in conversation. Volume 4 concentrates further on reading comprehension with its reading selections, utilizing the structures and vocabulary already learned together with new words, phrases, and structures. Numerous vocabulary words for passive learning are also introduced, some of which may become active vocabulary through repetition and repeated use.

The reading material has been carefully written to correlate with the material in the previous volumes; thus students should have little difficulty understanding this new material. In the beginning, the lessons are short, but they gradually become longer, as do the vocabulary lists, which should be used as references. The lessons are informative and should give the students a good general historical and cultural background of Japan that will enable the student better to understand and appreciate the Japan of today and its people as well as its language and culture.

We wish to thank former graduate students Anne Abe, Joanne Kodama, Dahleen Sawai, and Dean Yamato for their contributions and many hours of hard work. Mahalo.

SECTION I
GENERAL OBJECTIVES AND SUGGESTIONS

OBJECTIVES OF THE COURSE

1. Continue to develop and maintain self-confidence and a positive self-concept in speaking and understanding Japanese.
2. Continue to nurture and maintain a healthy attitude toward the Japanese people, their culture, and the language.
3. Continue to advance in the development of skills in oral and written communication.
4. Develop and expand skill in reading for information and/or pleasure.
5. Develop an understanding of Japanese history in order to appreciate present-day Japan.
6. Gain some knowledge and understanding of the economic and social problems of the Japanese today.
7. Develop understanding and appreciation of Japan's rapid progress and success in keeping up with the changing times.

AIDS IN TEACHING

This manual for Volume 4 provides suggestions for expanding the instructional activities for each lesson. Together with the drills and exercises in the text and exercise sheets, these activities provide students with ample opportunity to develop further their reading and listening comprehension as well as to continue their practice with speaking and writing. Additional information is provided to augment the content of each lesson. Further, the Appendixes provide (1) a list of video cassettes on all aspects of Japanese society (many of these may possibly be obtainable at a local Japanese Consulate), and (2) a reference list of useful books and periodicals.

SCHEDULING

The length of the class period will depend on class scheduling in each school. The lessons in this volume are designed for periods of at least fifty minutes, but adjustments to this schedule can be made by adding or deleting the suggested activities according to the needs of the students.

SECTION II
LESSON PRESENTATION AND PROCEDURES

LESSON FORMAT

The lessons in Volume 4 are primarily based on narratives for reading comprehension. Each lesson follows a standard format:

1. *Reading Selection.* A brief account of the major historical and cultural events in a given historical period.
2. *Vocabulary.* New words and expressions.
3. *Grammar.* New grammar points.
4. *Drills and Exercises.* Practice in reading and listening comprehension and in translation.
5. *Kanji.* New kanji, including their proper stroke order.

Many students learning Japanese expect to be functional in the language. Their major objective is first to be able to speak the language, and next to be able to read in the language for information and pleasure. Unfortunately, however, opportunities to speak Japanese outside the classroom are limited. Hence, reading may be one way to keep up with the newly acquired language. Therefore, Volume 4 has been prepared to help the student to develop this reading skill. Volumes 1 and 2 emphasized listening and speaking skills, and the reading selections and dialogues were basically for the reinforcement of what was learned audiolingually. Volume 3 introduced the written style and concentrated on the development of reading skills, while continuing to reinforce oral-aural skills as well. By the end of Volume 3, students should have acquired a good command of the relationship between sounds and graphic symbols, and between phrases and clauses in a sentence. Volume 4 now focuses on the development of this ability to interpret the meaning of a sentence by recognizing phrases and clauses and their relationships within the sentence structure, in order to comprehend the materials being read. Drills, exercises, and various activities have been prepared to help achieve this reading skill.

SUGGESTED PROCEDURE

1. Present the lesson narrative by reading it aloud. Students should listen and concentrate on the context (without looking at the text) to get a general idea of what is being read.
2. Ask general questions as to what the narrative is about.
3. Go over the new vocabulary and structures.
4. Go over each sentence for clarity of meaning. If necessary, especially with complex sentences, ask questions to elicit:
   a. the main or kernel sentence,
   b. the clauses that modify the main clause or sentence, and
   c. the phrases that modify the various clauses.

   The purpose of this type of exercise is to extract the meaning of each sentence.
5. Read again with the text open and the students following what is read to get the meaning of each paragraph.

6. Ask summarizing-type questions to check comprehension.
7. Have students read aloud for reading practice.
8. Have students read silently for comprehension, and have students discuss the interpretation of the narrative with partners.
9. Summarize orally the reading selection by eliciting answers to questions.
10. Have students write a summary of the selection.

INTRODUCTORY LESSON How to Use a Kanji Dictionary

KEY POINTS

The key point of this lesson is to familiarize students with the format and use of kanji dictionaries. Hence, it would be more meaningful for the students if each one has a dictionary to look at and work with and follows the steps in looking up a kanji character. This is also a good time to introduce the different kinds of dictionaries, such as the *Kokugo Jiten, Kojien, Akusento Jiten,* and *The Dictionary of Katakana Words,* and the way they are used.

ACTIVITY

Looking for Kanji in a Dictionary

Objective: To familiarize students with the format and usage of kanji dictionaries.

Materials: Japanese kanji dictionaries.

Procedure:

1. Review with students the steps for locating kanji in dictionaries.
2. Select kanji which contain frequently used radicals. Ex. 性、海、住.
3. Divide the class into two or more groups, depending upon the number of kanji dictionaries available.
4. Give a dictionary to one student in each group.
5. Write a kanji on the chalkboard and ask the student with the dictionary in each group to look it up.
6. The first student to give the correct reading and meaning of the character earns a point for his team.
7. The dictionary is then passed to another student in each group, and a new kanji is written on the chalkboard.
8. The group with the most points wins.

LESSON 1 Japan and Its Climate

I. KEY POINTS

A. *Grammar Notes*

1. (3) *Wa . . . ga*. What precedes *wa* is the topic of the sentence, and what precedes *ga* is the subject of the sentence and explains or describes the topic.
2. (5) Verb-*masu* stem + *hajimeru* (starting) or *owaru* (finishing). Note that only certain verbs can be used to make these compounds.

B. *Vocabulary*

II. ADDITIONAL INFORMATION

The Seasons

Japan has four distinct seasons. Each has its own beauty and charm. *Spring* is from March to May and is considered to be the most desirable season for tourists, because Japan is decorated with the cherry blossoms for which it is famous. From the latter part of March, in the south, through April and even into May in the north, Japan is covered with *sakura* or cherry blossoms. Spring is also favored by young people, because of a number of traditional festivities associated with the season's flowers. The Girl's Day festival or *Hinamatsuri* is celebrated on March 3 with peach blossoms, and the Boy's Day festival or *Tango no sekku* on May 5 with irises.

Spring is a time of *hana-mi,* blossom viewing, which is a natural excuse for a party. Many people picnic with friends and relatives when the *sakura* is in bloom, and *sake* parties often last far into the night under the illuminated cherry trees. Thus, one often hears *hana yori dango,* meaning "people enjoy partying more than the flower viewing" for which they originally gathered.

Summer, the warmest season, lasting from June to August, is a season of fresh greenness, warm air, and brilliant sunshine. The many seaside, mountain, and highland resorts offer a variety of outdoor sports and recreational activities, attracting numerous sports enthusiasts as well as refugees from the heat. Yachting, boating, fishing, mountaineering, and camping are popular summer pastimes. Summer is also a season of colorful festivities which include *Tanabata,* the Star Festival, annually held on July 7, and the *Bon* Festival, which begins on July 15.

Autumn offers cooler weather, a serene sky, and crisp air, which make for an ideal season for pleasant outings. This is a time for *momiji-gari,* maple-leaf viewing, in the countryside, which is covered with the tinted foliage of the maple trees, changing the mountains and valleys into brilliantly colored landscapes. The many varieties of chrysanthemums also come out in full glory at this time.

Autumn is also harvest time in Japan, and the golden rice fields cover the rural farming areas. During this season traditional festivals, sports gatherings, cultural functions, art exhibitions, musical entertainments, and chrysanthemum shows are observed in many parts of the country. Families often enjoy *tsuki-mi,* moon viewing, through the trees, under the beautiful October moon.

Winter in Japan is not very cold, except in the extreme north, with occasional sunshine and blue skies. Winter sports are very popular and are enjoyed by many at the ski grounds and winter resorts. Christmas and the New Year are celebrated with splendor and gaiety throughout the country. Other traditional events and religious rites take place from time to time. Where there is snow, one can enjoy *yuki-mi,* snow viewing, or huddle around the *kotatsu* table and enjoy a *nabe* meal.

Kotatsu

Traditionally, a *kotatsu* was a heating device that used charcoal to generate warmth. Charcoals were put in a fire-proof container (often set in the floor), over which a low, wooden frame was placed. This was often covered with a thickly padded quilt for added warmth.

Today, charcoal is no longer used, except perhaps in rural areas of Japan. Instead, an electric heating device is attached to the bottom of a low table. A soft thick quilt known as a *kakebuton* is placed over the table. *Kotatsu* users place their legs and often their arms under the covers. Japanese enjoy talking, watching TV, studying, and/or eating *mikan* (tangerines) while sitting next to the *kotatsu* during the cold winter months.

In space-conscious Japan, today's *kotatsu* is very convenient in that it can be unplugged, folded up, and stored away when not in use. It may also be converted into a regular Japanese table by removing the quilt.

Nabe-mono

Nabe refers to a pot, pan, or saucepan. Hence, *nabe-mono* is a type of dish that is cooked in a pot or saucepan, using meat, fish, or chicken, along with *tofu* (soybean curd) and vegetables. While this may not seem very unusual, what is special about *nabe-mono* is that the cooking is done right at the dining table. Family members and friends seat themselves around the table and eat directly from the pot while the *nabe-mono* is cooking. As the vegetables, *tofu,* fish, and so forth are eaten, more are added to the simmering broth so that they can be continuously eaten piping hot. Thus, *nabe-mono* is a favorite among the Japanese during the cold winter months.

These are various types of *nabe-mono.* A few examples are:

1. *Sukiyaki* (see Volume 2, Lesson 10, Teacher's Manual).
2. *Yose-nabe* is a traditional Japanese dish cooked in a pot at the table. It usually contains chicken, fish, shellfish, *tofu,* and vegetables, and is cooked in soup seasoned with fish stock, sweet rice wine, soy sauce, and so forth.
3. *Mizu-taki* is another type of *nabe* dish in which chicken, *tofu,* and vegetables are cooked in a chicken or fish stock. When cooking is done, each person scoops chunks of chicken, *tofu,* and vegetables along with the soup into a small bowl. These are then eaten with a combination of *ponzu* sauce (made from lemon juice or vinegar), soy sauce, and other condiments such as grated Japanese radish *(daikon)* and ginger.

Tsuyu

Tsuyu or *baiu* refers to the rainy season, which occurs from mid-June to mid-July.

Taifuu

The typhoon, known as *taifuu,* is almost an annual occurrence. Every autumn a strong storm strikes somewhere with results that are so familiar, especially in southern Japan, that the newspapers could almost use the same reports every year, changing only the proper names and the casualty figures.

Taue

Taue refers to the transplanting of rice seedlings from the nursery to the rice fields, which occurs in June during *baiu.* Wet-rice farming is the cultivating of rice in patchworks of small plots, each surrounded by steep earthen walls and watered by a common irrigation system.

ACTIVITY 1

Finding the Main Idea in a Sentence

Objective: To practice finding the main idea in a sentence.

Material: Textbook.

Procedure:

1. Have the students read a sentence silently; then have them answer the questions that follow.

   Ex. *Nihon zentai no ookisa wa Amerika no Kariforunia shuu to onaji gurai desu.*

   Q: What is the main idea in this sentence?
   A: *Nihon wa Kariforunia shuu to onaji gurai desu.*

   Q: What part of Japan is the same as California?
   A: *Nihon zentai no ookisa.*

2. Ask what, where, when, and why questions, to elicit clauses that modify the main sentence.
3. Have the students repeat the whole sentence to see the relationship of the various modifying clauses to the kernel sentence.

Sample questions, using the procedure just given:

a. *Hachigatsu no owari goro kara aki kaze ga fukihajimemasu.*

b. *Aki no owari goro ni naru to, kiku no hana ga sakimasu.*

c. *Aki wa shuukaku no kisetsu de, iroiro na kudamono ga minorimasu.*

ACTIVITY 2

Kanji Search

Objective: To have students find kanji that have appeared in previous lessons, give their meanings, and/or make kanji compounds.

Ex. *Shima, kuni:* island country.

Materials: Japanese magazines and newspapers, scissors, glue/paste, paper, pencil, a timer.

Procedure:

1. Pass out magazines and newspapers.
2. Tell students they will be given thirty minutes in which to find any kanji and okurigana learned thus far, cut them out, glue or paste them on a sheet of paper, and write their meanings. Dictionaries may be used as a last resort.
3. Set timer to thirty minutes and tell class to begin.
4. When time is up, collect papers.
5. Check and grade papers.
6. Return papers to students and have them file them in their folders.

Variation: This could be made into a game with teams.

ACTIVITY 3

Kanji on Overhead Projector

Objective: To have students see, read, and learn the meaning of kanji.

Materials: Transparencies, overhead projector.

Procedure:

1. List new kanji on transparencies.
2. Flash transparencies on a screen for reading practice.
3. Have students make sentences with kanji.

Variation: This can be either an oral or a written exercise.

ACTIVITY 4

Story in Strips (Narrative Sequence)

Objective: To test comprehension skills by having students put sentences into a correct sequence.

Materials: Strips of paper.

Procedure:

1. Divide the class into groups of eight.
2. Using the eight sentences below, copy each sentence on a separate strip of paper.
3. Give a complete set of strips to each group—one strip to each student in a group. Have each student memorize the sentence that he or she has received.
4. Collect the strips. On a signal, have the students in each group recite their sentences and try to come up with a story with all sentences in proper sequence.
5. The team that finishes first wins.

Eight sentences to be put in proper sequence:

a. Nihon rettoo ni wa juuman nen ijoo mae kara ningen ga sunde ita to iwarete imasu ga, san, yon seiki goro ni wa, Nihon to iuu kuni wa mada arimasendeshita.

b. Ikutsuka no dokuritsu shita shizoku ga atte, otagai ni arasotte ita no desu.

c. Sono uchi ni Yamato chihoo ni ita gozoku ga ta no shizoku o horoboshi, shidai ni tsuyoku nari, ookiku natte ikimashita.

d. Sono koro no seikatsu wa hijoo ni kantan de, yama ya kaigan de uo o tottari, noogyoo o shitarishite imashita.

e. Kome ga juuyoona sakumotsu deshita.

f. Shuukyoo wa shizen suuhai deshita.

g. Hitobito wa ookina ki, iwa, kawa, yama, ten, chi, taiyoo nado, daishizen no subarashi mono wa nan demo ogamimashita.

h. Sore ga shintoo no hajimari desu.

LESSON 2 Japan before the Advent of Buddhist Culture

I. KEY POINTS

A. *Grammar Notes*

1. (1) *Nan demo,* meaning "anything."

2. (3) "Not A, but B," expressed by A . . . *naku,* B . . . *desu.*

3. (4) Verb-*ta* form used as a noun modifier.

4. (6) *Yoo ni naru* used to mean that the old situation has changed to a new one.

B. *Vocabulary*

C. *Nature Worship*

II. ADDITIONAL INFORMATION

Shinto

Shinto is the indigenous religion of Japan, with no dogma, no moral code, and no historical founder. Its chief feature is the worship of nature, ancestors, and ancient national heroes. Shinto was Japan's state religion from 1867 to 1945, and the many shrines were supported by the government until before the end of World War II. Today, however, they are maintained by offerings and donations.

Ise Jinguu

Ise Jinguu consists of two shrines, the Naikuu (Inner Shrine) and the Gekuu (Outer Shrine). The Naikuu is said to be dedicated to Amaterasu Oomikami, the Sun Goddess, while the Gekuu is dedicated to Toyouke Oomikami, the goddess of the farms, the harvest, food, and sericulture. The Ise shrines have been demolished and rebuilt on adjacent lots in a ceremonial event that takes place every twenty years, with the last ceremony having taken place in October 1973.

Izumo Taisha

The Izumo Shrine, located on the Japan Sea coast, is the oldest center of Shinto worship, and it is said that various symbols of the Imperial Family are kept here. Rebuilt periodically until 1744, this shrine has faithfully retained the tradition of the *taisha zukuri,* a style of Shinto architecture which dates back to prehistoric times.

Two important rituals of worship at the shrine are the *harai* and the *misogi,* which reflect the Japanese insistence on cleanliness. *Harai* refers to the sweeping out of a house and the special rites of chasing away evil spirits; *misogi* refers to the washing of the body, an act of increasing spiritual significance.

Amaterasu Oomikami

Amaterasu Oomikami, the Sun Goddess, is believed to be the ancestor of the Imperial Family. She is enshrined in the Inner Shrine of the Grand Shrine of Ise, which was erected in her honor. She is regarded as the national deity of Japan.

ACTIVITY 1

Finding the Main Idea in a Sentence

Procedure:

Have the students read a sentence silently, then find the main idea in the sentence, using the following sentences.

a. 米が重要な作物でした。

b. それぞれの氏族のチーフは神の子孫であると、人々は信じていました。

c. やまと氏族のリーダーは天皇で、天皇はたくさんの神々の中で一番重要なあまてらすおおみかみという神の子孫であると人々は信じていました。

d. この時代にはまだ文字がありませんでしたから、人々は読むことや書くことはできませんでした。

ACTIVITY 2

Paragraph Scramble

Objective: To have students be able to understand a passage and arrange sentences in proper sequence.

Materials: Strips of paper.

Procedure:

1. Divide the class into three groups of five or more students each.
2. Select paragraphs from the lesson narrative, and write the sentences from each paragraph on strips of paper.
3. Gather the strips for each paragraph, and put each set into a separate box.
4. Assign a box with strips to each group (the number of students should equal the number of sentences in a box).
5. Have each student pick a sentence from the box assigned to his or her group.
6. Have each group get together for five minutes to work out the proper sequence of the sentences in the box.
7. Have each group present the resulting paragraph.
8. Give points to the group(s) with perfect scores.

Students not assigned to a group can make corrections, if necessary.

ACTIVITY 3

Kanji Drill

Objective: To master the newly introduced kanji.

Procedure:

1. Divide the class into teams.
2. Call out a kanji.

3. Have any student from each team run up to the board and write the kanji.
4. The student who writes the kanji correctly first—using the proper stroke order—earns a point for his team.

ACTIVITY 4

Kanji Compound Games (A)

Objective: To have students learn kanji compounds.

Materials: 3 × 5 inch cards.

Procedure:

1. On 3 × 5 inch flash cards, write individual kanji.
2. Have the students move the cards around freely so that they can look for as many kanji compounds as possible.

This can be an individual assignment or a group activity involving teams that compete with each other.

Kanji Compound Games (B)

Objective: To construct as many compound words as possible.

Materials: Paper, cardboard, and access to a ditto or photocopy machine.

Procedure:

1. Prepare masters for ditto or photocopy by writing kanji on 3 × 5 inch cards. Cut out the copies and paste on cardboard backing (now you have several sets of kanji cards).
2. Present each kanji to the whole class.
3. After the students have had thorough exposure to each kanji, divide the class into small groups of five to eight students each.
4. Deal the cards. Have students take turns, each asking another for a card that he or she needs to make a kanji compound. If the student fails to get the card requested, then the student loses a turn. If the card is obtained, the student continues until he or she fails to obtain the desired card.
5. The student with the most compounds wins the most points.

LESSON 3 The Importing of Chinese Culture

I. KEY POINTS

A. *Grammar Notes*

1. (1) *Mo,* meaning "even that," replacing the subject or object particle.
2. (2) *Made ni,* meaning "by," following a time word.
3. (3) *O . . . ni suru,* meaning "to have someone take a position" or "change one thing to another."

B. *Vocabulary*

C. *Introduction of Buddhism*

D. *Introduction of Chinese Writing*

II. ADDITIONAL INFORMATION

Shotoku Taishi

Prince Shotoku is one of the greatest figures of Japanese history, especially because of his efforts in the propagation of Buddhism. He was a follower of the teachings of Eiji, a monk of Koma (Korea), and as soon as he came to power, he selected three sutras of the Mahayana doctrine and ordered them to be taught everywhere. He was responsible for the erection of many temples, and by the time of his death, there had been established forty-six Buddhist *tera* or temples, with 820 monks and 560 nuns in Japan. Shotoku Taishi was the first to send an embassy to China, in 607, and to adopt the Chinese calendar.

Buddhism

The teachings of Buddhism were first preached by Shaka (557–477 B.C.). A thousand years later, in A.D. 550, Buddhist statues and books were presented to Emperor Kimmei by the king of Korea. Two years afterwards, two monks named Tonei and Doshin arrived in Japan to preach the Buddhist religion.

The ultimate goal in Buddhism is to attain enlightenment through the understanding and practice of Buddhist teachings. Buddhism teaches correct living and self-denial, which will enable the soul to reach nirvana, a divine state of release from bodily pain and sorrow.

Tera or Temples

The appearance of temples throughout Japan may be thought of as an indication of the great influence Buddhism has had on Japanese culture. Buddhist images are enshrined within a Buddhist temple, where monks live together, studying the Buddhist teachings. The size of a temple compound may vary from a single structure to a large complex.

Horyuji

The edifice of Horyuji Temple is perhaps the most indicative of the nature of the Asuka culture; it is also the oldest wooden structure in the world. The original structure dated back to the early seventh century (A.D. 607) and is said to have been the headquarters of the Shotoku sect. Unfortunately, it was destroyed by fire in A.D. 670, and so it is the reconstructed edifice that we see today. The present edifice exhibits the distinctive characteristics of Asuka architecture, and in it are preserved numerous examples of Buddhist sculpture from that period.

ACTIVITY 1

Finding the Main Idea in a Sentence

Procedure:

Have the students read a sentence silently, then find the main idea in the sentence, using the sentences below.

a. 六世紀の終わりごろ日本をおさめていた聖徳太子は中国の文化を日本に取り入れました。

b. 奈良にある法隆寺という寺は世界で最も古い木造建築として有名ですが、これは、仏教を広めるために聖徳太子によって建てられたと伝えられています。

c. 兄は子供の時からあたまがよくて、学校のせいせきもいつもAだったが、口がおもいから、女の友だちがいなかった。

d. 朝からさむいさむいと思っていたが、とうとう雨がゆきに変わった。

ACTIVITY 2

Doing Research

Objective: To have students practice writing sentences in Japanese.

Procedure:

1. Assign students to do research in advance on Shotoku Taishi.
2. Have the students individually write a short paragraph in Japanese, including the answers to the following questions:
   a. Who was Shotoku Taishi?
   b. What were his accomplishments?
   c. What is the connection between Shotoku Taishi and the Horyuji?

ACTIVITY 3

Kanji Review Game

Objective: To stimulate kanji recognition, and to provide kanji reading and writing practice.

Procedure:

1. From previous lessons, select kanji that can be used to form a variety of compounds.
2. Taking each kanji out of context (that is, breaking up the compounds and writing the kanji individually), write the kanji in rows on the chalkboard. For example:

肉　一　何　人
度　夕　万　屋
番　年　牛　食

3. Divide the class into groups of three or four students each.
4. Give each group about ten minutes to form as many compounds as possible. Remind students that each kanji must be used at least once and that the words formed must make sense.
5. When time is up, have each group read off their list of compounds. The group with the largest number of legitimate compounds wins.

Variation: This may also be done as an individual exercise. Kanji worksheets can be passed out as homework or as an in-class activity. In addition to writing out the compounds, students should also be asked to write the furigana and English meanings for the compounds they have created. This may be corrected by the teacher, or the students may correct each other's work.

LESSON 4 The Nara Period

I. KEY POINTS

A. *Grammar Notes*

1. (1) *To iu,* which explains the word or phrase that follows.

B. *Vocabulary*

C. *The Spread of Buddhism*

II. ADDITIONAL INFORMATION

The Imperial Family

It is alleged that the beginning of the Imperial Family can be dated back to 660 B.C. with the reign of the legendary Emperor Jimmu, and the family has continued in a direct line to the present day, with Akihito as the 125th emperor.

Up until the Nara period (710–784), the imperial family wielded both political and military power, but during the Heian period (794–1192), this power was taken away from the emperor and it was never fully recovered.

Haiku

The structure of Japanese poetry has been determined by the nature of the language: every syllable (except one) ends in a simple vowel sound. Therefore, Japanese verses came to be based on the syllable count, and different types of poetry are usually distinguished by the number of syllables they contain.

The haiku, a more recent development, contains seventeen syllables in lines of five, seven, and five syllables. Although there is no great difficulty in composing a verse with only seventeen syllables, it is difficult to write something of aesthetic value. Also, the shortness of the poem limits the range of this type of poetry.

Masaoka Shiki

Shiki (1867–1902) is considered to be the poet who revived the haiku, which had begun to decline since the early 1700s. Shiki studied calligraphy and Chinese literature from an early age. He entered a high school in Tokyo at seventeen, and the following year he began to compose haiku without a teacher. In 1892 he began working for the Nippon Newspaper Company and established a new school of *haikai* (haiku). Shiki published several books, many articles, and a periodical called *Hototogisu* (cuckoo). He had suffered from pulmonary disease since his youth, and died at the early age of thirty-six.

ACTIVITY I

Kanji Practice: Dictation

Objective: To have students write sentences in Japanese using as many kanji as possible.

Procedure:

1. Read the sentences below out loud, repeating twice.
2. Have students write the sentence in Japanese with the underlined words in kanji.

a. 六世紀の終わりごろ日本の国をおさめていた聖徳太子は中国の文化を日本に取り入れました。

b. 六世紀の終わりごろまでには漢字や仏教も入って来ました。

c. 奈良にある法隆寺という寺は世界で最も古い木造建築として有名です。

d. 日本の気候は四季の変化がはっきりしています。

e. 木々の葉が落ちてしまうと、もう冬です。

f. そのころの生活は非常に簡単で、川や海岸で魚を取ったり、農業をしたりしていました。

g. それぞれの神が大自然の力のシンボルだったのです。

h. 天皇は仏教の力で人々の不安を静めようとしました。

i. 天皇は約70年間続いた奈良の都をすてて、794年に今の京都に平安京という新しい都を造りました。

ACTIVITY 2

Listening Comprehension Practice

Objective: To check the students' comprehension of what they hear.

Procedure:

1. Choose sentences at random and read aloud.
2. Have students give the meaning of the sentences.

Variation 1: Read a paragraph twice, and have students summarize the idea of the paragraph.

Variation 2: Distribute a paragraph written in Japanese, with questions on the paragraph. Have the students answer the questions. Below is a sample paragraph.

日本の四つの島のうちで、北海道が一番北で、九州が一番南にあります。北海道という所は冬はとてもさむくてスキーができます。そしてスキーのできる山のそばには町がたくさんあります。だから週末には東京からもスキーをしに来る人がたくさんいます。

ACTIVITY 3

Reading Comprehension Practice

Objective: To test the students' reading proficiency.

Materials: Handouts, timer.

Procedure:

1. Prepare a handout consisting of a paragraph (with reading material familiar to the students) and blanks to be filled in.
2. Distribute the handout, give a signal to start, and set timer for twenty minutes.
3. Collect and grade the papers.

ACTIVITY 4

Kanji Stroke Order Game

Objective: To test students' knowledge of kanji.

Materials: List of all kanji learned thus far, chalkboard, chalk.

Procedure:

1. Divide class into teams.
2. Select kanji (including compounds) from the list and call them out.
3. Have one member at a time from each team go to the chalkboard and write one stroke of the kanji until the kanji is completed (the strokes must be in proper sequence).
4. The first team to complete a kanji correctly earns one point.

ACTIVITY 5

Write a Haiku

Objective: To encourage students to express themselves creatively in Japanese by writing simple poetry.

Procedure:

1. Have each student write a haiku, in Japanese, following the 5-7-5 syllable form (allow 10–15 minutes).
2. Have the students pair up and share their haiku with their partners, analyzing and discussing the meanings of their haiku.

LESSON 5 The Heian Period (A): The Life of the Aristocrats

I. KEY POINTS

A. *Grammar Notes*

1. (1) *Shootai suru* preceded by the particle *ni,* after a word meaning an event to which an invitation is made.

2. (2) The particle *ga* connecting two statements not contrary to each other, meaning "and" (rather than "but").

B. *Vocabulary*

C. *The Life of the Aristocrats*

II. ADDITIONAL INFORMATION

The Heian Period

Japan's first permanent capital was established in Nara in A.D. 710. After a few decades, it was abandoned and a new capital was built at Heian (today's Kyoto). Spanning almost four centuries, the Heian period was an important era in Japanese history.

During the Nara period, Japanese civilization was heavily influenced by elements of Chinese culture. This Chinese cultural influence remained strong in the early years of the Heian period. For example, it was at this time that two important sects of Buddhism (the Tendai and Shingon sects) were introduced into Japan from China. Buddhism, which has had a significant influence on the Japanese down through the centuries, was first developed and "domesticated" during the Heian period.

Japan cut its ties with China early in the period, and the Japanese turned their back on Chinese civilization, concentrating instead on developing a culture indigenous to Japan. The result of this was a blossoming of Japanese art, architecture, and literature.

During the ninth century, hiragana and katakana, the two syllabaries used in modern Japanese writing, were developed in response to the growing desire to create poetry and prose in Japanese. Until then, cumbersome Chinese characters had been used. With the birth of a native writing system capable of capturing the nuances and subtleties of the Japanese language, magnificent prose compositions began to emerge in the early eleventh century. Among the literary works produced during this period was Lady Murasaki's *Tale of Genji,* still one of Japan's greatest literary creations.

Uji

Uji is a city located south of Kyoto. Situated on the bank of the Uji River, it is considered a very fashionable resort area. Uji is noted for its beautiful scenery, Buddhist temples, Shinto shrines, and historical relics as well as for its high-quality green tea.

ACTIVITY I

Making Individual Vocabulary Flashcards

Objective: To review old vocabulary.

Materials: 5 × 8 inch index cards (may be cut lengthwise into two).

Procedure:

1. Pass out index cards to students.

2. Have students write out vocabulary that they still do not know, from all the lessons studied thus far, for later self-study (allow 15 minutes).

This activity can be repeated from time to time, so that students can add new words to their flashcard file.

ACTIVITY 2

Glossing of Unfamiliar Words

Objective: To learn to determine the meaning of words by reading in context and glossing.

Materials: Reading Selection, transparencies, overhead projector.

Procedure:

1. Prepare overhead transparencies with material from the Reading Selection, in Japanese.
2. Project a transparency, and allow time for students to read the paragraph on the screen.
3. Ask what the paragraph says.
4. Have students answer who, what, when, where, and why questions.
5. Ask which words are new to the students.
6. Tell the students to go back over the paragraph and guess at the meanings of the unfamiliar words in relation to what they think the paragraph is about. (This is to be done orally, for all the words the students do not know.)
7. Check to see whether the students' guesses fit into the meaning of the paragraph (also to be done orally).
8. Repeat this procedure with the next paragraph.

Suggested paragraphs:

建築

奈良の大仏の近くの山の上に子供たちの遊園地ドリーム・ランドを作ろうとした時、奈良の人々をはじめ、新聞、雑誌などのマスコミが騒いだ。京都の駅前に近代的な京都タワーが建てられることになった時も、日本中の人々が驚き、反対した。奈良も京都も古い寺や神社、族館や料理屋などが多く、落ち着いた日本的なふん囲気が残っているので、人々はそれをこわしたくなかったからである。

しかし、ドリーム・ランドは遊ぶ場所の少なくなった子供の娯楽場として、その後、人気が出て来たし、子供が行きたがるので、親もいっしょに出かけることになり、おかげで、週末など、いつも満員になった。京都タワーの方も、ふしぎにまわりとよく調和し、観光客にも評判がよく、文句を言う人もだんだん少なくなった。

ACTIVITY 3

Excursion to a Temple (for localities where there is access to a Buddhist temple)

Objective: To familiarize students with the architecture and contents of a Buddhist temple.

Procedure:

1. Make arrangements with the temple in advance.
2. Before the excursion, briefly present a background talk on the temple and its history.
3. Should there be a priest, monk, or official guide attached to the temple, inquire if he might be able to explain the various paintings and objects in or near the altar, as well as the history of the temple itself.

ACTIVITY 4

Developing Games

Objective: To have students apply what they have learned.

Procedure:

1. Ask students to apply what they have learned in class to a game that they know—or to make up a game using what they have learned in class (set a time limit).
2. If the students are not finished when the teacher calls time, have them continue the activity outside of class time.

Play the games in class to test their usefulness for drills or review.

LESSON 6 The Heian Period (B): From Chinese Civilization to Japanese Civilization

I. KEY POINTS

A. *Grammar Notes*

1. (1) *Akogareru* taking the particle *ni* after the word or phrase that indicates the object of yearning.
2. (2) The difference between *kara* + *tsukuru* ("is made from") and *de* + *tsukuru* ("is made from").
3. (4) *Ni* used after a nominal, indicating state or place to which something is moved, transferred, or changed.

B. *Vocabulary*

C. *History of Hiragana and Katakana Writing*

II. ADDITIONAL INFORMATION

Genji Monogatari

The sudden flowering of literature in the Heian period can be attributed to the invention of the kana syllabary, which enabled the Japanese to express their feelings more effectively.

The most outstanding example of this literary output is the *Genji monogatari (The Tale of Genji),* written by a court lady named Murasaki Shikibu. It is a novel that describes the magnificence surrounding the love affairs of the aristocracy. However, beneath the superficial events of the narrative there is an undercurrent of philosophical awareness of the transitoriness of life. *The Tale of Genji* continues to live as a poignant memorial to the fleeting world of the Heian aristocracy.

Waka

Waka is a general term for the classical Japanese verse form that was developed in the Heian period. It quickly became the most appropriate medium for the expression of refined aristocratic sensitivity and perceptivity.

Juuni Hitoe

The *juuni hitoe* was a ceremonial costume worn by court ladies in the Heian period. It consisted of twelve unlined robes, worn one layer over another, with the emphasis on the complex beauty at the collar and sleeve openings. Today this costume is worn by the imperial princesses at their weddings.

Japanese Penmanship and the Origin of the Kana Syllabary

Japanese kanji penmanship has different styles, including the *kaisho,* the *gyoosho,* and the *soosho.* The *kaisho* is the square style, in which each stroke is written clearly without slighting even one dot. The *gyoosho* is the more simplified style that is very practical and the one most commonly used in writing. The *soosho* ("grass writing") style is even more simplified; it is quite different from the square *kaisho* style and is often quite difficult to read unless one examines the characters carefully, or has previously studied this style of writing.

All of the symbols in the hiragana and katakana phonetic scripts are derived originally from Chinese characters. In the first set of groupings below can be seen (a) the original characters from which the kana are derived, and (b) the three different styles of penmanship. In each group, the *first* column on the left shows the modern kana symbol; the *second* column shows the kanji from which that kana was derived, with the kanji written in *kaisho* style; the *third* column shows the same kanji in *gyoosho* style; and the *fourth* column shows the kanji in *soosho* style.

The hiragana syllabary and its derivation:

あ 安 安 あ
い 以 以 い
う 宇 宇 う
え 衣 衣 え
お 於 於 お

か 加 加 か
き 幾 幾 き
く 久 久 く
け 計 計 け
こ 己 己 こ

さ 左 左 さ
し 之 之 し
す 寸 寸 す
せ 世 世 せ
そ 曽 曽 そ

た 太 太 た
ち 知 知 ち
つ 川 川 つ
て 天 天 て
と 止 止 と

な 奈 奈 な
に 仁 仁 に
ぬ 奴 奴 ぬ
ね 祢 祢 ね
の 乃 乃 の

は 波 波 は
ひ 比 比 ひ
ふ 不 不 ふ
へ 部 部 へ
ほ 保 保 ほ

ま 末 末 ま
み 美 美 み
む 武 武 む
め 女 女 め
も 毛 毛 も

や 也 也 や
ゆ 由 由 ゆ
よ 与 与 よ

ら 良 良 ら
り 利 利 り
る 留 留 る
れ 禮 禮 れ
ろ 呂 呂 ろ

わ 和 和 わ
を 遠 遠 を
ん 无 无 ん

Calligraphy by Hiromi N. Peterson (Tohka Nakai)

Next, the katakana syllabary, with the modern katakana in the first column of each group, and the Chinese character from which each katakana was derived, in the second column:

ア	阿	カ	加	サ	散	タ	多
イ	伊	キ	幾	シ	之	チ	千
ウ	宇	ク	久	ス	須	ツ	川
エ	江	ケ	介	セ	世	テ	天
オ	於	コ	己	ソ	曽	ト	止
ナ	奈	ハ	八	マ	万	ヤ	也
ニ	二	ヒ	比	ミ	三	ユ	由
ヌ	奴	フ	不	ム	牟	ヨ	与
ネ	祢	ヘ	部	メ	女		
ノ	乃	ホ	保	モ	毛		
ラ	良	ワ	和				
リ	利	ヲ	乎				
ル	流	ン	尓				
レ	礼						
ロ	呂						

Calligraphy by Hiromi N. Peterson (Tohka Nakai)

ACTIVITY I

Reading Comprehension

Objective: To have students read and guess at the meaning and content of an article.

Materials: Short articles or other features from a magazine or newspaper.

Procedure:

1. Pass out material for students to read.
2. Allow time for students to read the material silently.
3. Ask questions about the material: What is the material about? What phrases or words provide clues to the subject? Can you tell what happens?

ACTIVITY 2

A Day at the Newspaper Company (Skit)

Objective: To introduce the different sections of a Japanese newspaper.

Materials: Copies of a Japanese newspaper.

Procedure:

1. Talk to the class about the different sections of a newspaper.
2. Pass out a newspaper and have the students become familiar with it.
3. Tell the class to prepare for the presentation of a skit, "A Day at the Newspaper Company." It will be a class activity to be presented in Japanese, at a later date.
4. Assign roles, such as reporters, editors, and press operators.
5. Have students meet in groups outside class to practice.

ACTIVITY 3

Word-Find

Objective: To review and reinforce learned vocabulary.

Materials: Copies of a puzzle with clues, like the sample provided here.

Procedure:

1. Select vocabulary from the lessons studied thus far.
2. Create a puzzle (like the one shown for this activity), with the selected vocabulary embedded in the puzzle (the items may appear horizontally, vertically, or diagonally). In a separate list, put the English translations or clues.
3. Have the students complete the exercise by: (a) translating the English words provided into Japanese, and (b) finding the Japanese words in the puzzle.

Clues for the puzzle:

1. admire; long for
2. widely
3. express
4. novel
5. modern (Japanese) language
6. Lady Murasaki
7. spread; move; shift
8. translation
9. tale
10. for instance; for example
11. Chinese literature
12. woman; lady; girl
13. part; section
14. simplify
15. kana characters
16. sentiment; feeling; emotion
17. essay; notes
18. the original
19. clothing; dress
20. come to flourish
21. man; boy
22. depicted; described

Puzzle

1	む	た	ゆ	く	ふ	う	ね	に	あ	ひ	こ	よ
2	ら	と	る	ず	い	ひ	つ	れ	こ	い	り	て
3	さ	く	に	す	え	ょ	ぶ	る	さ	ず	ん	だ
4	き	か	ゃ	ね	か	う	か	つ	の	お	い	う
5	し	な	ん	だ	め	げ	は	ん	あ	さ	し	ふ
6	き	も	く	に	さ	ん	ん	し	ぶ	き	ぬ	す
7	ぶ	じ	の	そ	な	す	え	ぶ	ぶ	ん	み	お
8	ち	あ	こ	が	れ	る	へ	だ	ん	し	が	ご
9	ら	う	た	く	た	ぬ	す	の	づ	し	ょ	く
10	た	な	に	こ	の	り	ふ	ら	ひ	ら	ほ	ね
11	は	け	か	ほ	そ	え	こ	い	た	と	え	ば
12	き	ば	ひ	ん	せ	ち	ふ	い	お	れ	が	じ
13	も	こ	て	や	じ	す	く	げ	ん	だ	い	ご
14	ん	ひ	ろ	く	ょ	ょ	そ	ず	か	あ	た	と
15	や	く	ち	え	し	ょ	う	せ	つ	も	き	ん
	1	2	3	4	5	6	7	8	9	10	11	12

Answer key to puzzle

	1	2	3	4	5	6	7	8	9	10	11	12
1	む			く		う						
2	ら			ず	い	ひ	つ					
3	さ			す		ょ		る				
4	き	か				う	か					
5	し	な	ん			げ		ん				
6	き	も		に		ん	ん		ぶ			
7	ぶ	じ	の		な	す		ぶ	ぶ	ん		
8		あ	こ	が	れ	る		だ	ん	し	が	
9					た							く
10						り						
11			か	ほ					た	と	え	ば
12				ん			ふ				が	
13				や	じ		く	げ	ん	だ	い	ご
14		ひ	ろ	く	ょ	ょ	そ				た	
15					し	ょ	う	せ	つ			

ACTIVITY 4

Shiritori (Word-ending game)

Objective: To enable students to recognize the different sounds of the Japanese syllabary.

Procedure:

1. Divide the class into two teams.
2. To one of the teams, give a first word—for example, *"Furansugo."*
3. Have the first member of team 1 think of another word that begins with the last syllable *"go,"* such as *"gohan."*
4. If the student answers correctly, then his or her team continues the game, with the next member of the team.
5. If the student does not answer correctly within a certain time limit, then a point goes to the other team.
6. In the case of a word that ends in *"n"* (like *"gohan"*), then the team must respond with a completely different word.

LESSON 7 The Kamakura and Ashikaga Periods

I. KEY POINTS

A. *Grammar Notes*

1. (1) *Donna ni . . . -temo (demo),* meaning "no matter how . . ." or "even if . . ."

2. (3) *Ni* replaced by a *comma* after a time word.

B. *Vocabulary*

C. *The Beginning of the Shogunate*

II. ADDITIONAL INFORMATION

Minamoto-no-Yoritomo

Minamoto-no-Yoritomo is known to have formed a military protectorate over the entire country. His establishment of the Shogunate in 1185 in Kamakura was not a usurpation of the emperor's authority, for it had received the sanction of the imperial system. Yoritomo strove to build this military power, and it later led to his acquisition of court honors, titles, and ultimate legitimacy. His military headquarters was located in Kamakura and later grew to take on the character of an administrative center. Yoritomo was a major power within both the civil and the military centers of government by the time he became Shogun.

Ashikaga Takauji

Ashikaga Takauji was a military leader who captured Kyoto for Emperor Go-Daigo during a period of political unrest. After turning against the emperor in 1335, Takauji proceeded to establish his own government, and in 1338 he acquired the title of Shogun. Under the advice of his chief spiritual advisor, he established the monastery Tenryuuji, in memory of the by-then deceased Emperor Go-Daigo.

Nichiren Buddhism

Nichiren is a sect of Buddhism that was established by the monk Nichiren (1222–1282) during the Kamakura period, a time of much strife in Japan. Nichiren came to believe that he was the only person who could save Japan from ruin, through his own interpretation of Buddhism. He taught his followers that all truth was revealed in the Mahayana Buddhist sutra, *The Sutra of the Lotus of the Good Law.* According to the followers of Nichiren, the saying or chanting of the *Lotus Sutra* was an important act of faith, and followers today can often be heard chanting the invocation *"Namu myoohoo renge kyoo."*

Zen Buddhism

Zen, a form of Buddhism that was preferred by samurai warriors, was introduced from China in the early Kamakura period. In this new Buddhist sect, meditation and the ideals of simplicity and closeness to nature were emphasized. The samurai found the strict life of the Zen monasteries appealing, and they saw the rigorous self-discipline of the practice of Zen meditation as a way to develop the self-control and firmness of character that their way of life demanded. Zen monasteries around Kamakura and Kyoto became the great intellectual centers of medieval Japan and had the support of the feudal leaders. In the late medieval period, Zen Buddhism incorporated a whole aesthetic system that became a lasting element of Japanese culture. The small, the simple, the natural, and even the misshapen were valued over the large, the grand, the artificial, and the uniform.

ACTIVITY 1

Introduction to Reading a Newspaper

Objective: To teach words found in a newspaper and test the students' comprehension of them.

Materials: Newspaper reading material, newspaper-compound dictionary.

Procedure:

1. Read over a recent edition of a Japanese newspaper, and select an item or items for copying.
2. Present the selection to the class.
3. Have students read the selection and then discuss and answer questions on it.

Variation: Have the class listen to a taped news broadcast. Then have a discussion, to include questions and answers.

ACTIVITY 2

Newspaper Kanji Compounds

Objective: To learn the meanings and readings of kanji compounds found in a newspaper.

Materials: Japanese newspaper, kanji dictionary.

Procedure:

1. Have students look over a newspaper and pick out four or five unfamiliar kanji compounds, and have them look up the meanings and readings in a kanji dictionary (both for the compounds and for the individual kanji).
2. Hold a class discussion on some of these kanji, to include the following questions:
   a. What are the separate meanings of the kanji in a compound?
   b. Does each kanji give a clue to the meaning of the compound, or are the individual meanings different from the meaning of the compound?
   c. Are there any compounds not found in the dictionary?
   d. Can you guess the meaning from the context of the newspaper article?

ACTIVITY 3

Cultural Presentation (A): Waka

Objective: To provide students with a better understanding of Japanese culture through a discussion of a literary art.

Procedure:

1. Introduce the students to famous or interesting *waka* (this can be done by the teacher, or by having the students select their own, or by inviting a guest speaker to give a talk).
2. Have the students write their own *waka,* in either English or Japanese.

Cultural Presentation (B): Tea Ceremony or Ikebana

Objective: To provide students with a better understanding of Japanese culture through a discussion of a ceremonial or decorative art.

Procedure:

1. Put on a demonstration of these traditional art forms for the students (a cultural-resource person could be invited to do this for the class).
2. Encourage the students to participate in the live demonstration.
3. Hold a discussion on the history of these art forms and their relevance to Japanese society.

ACTIVITY 4

Research Project (A): Historical Figures

Objective: To have students learn more about the early historical figures of Japan.

Have the students do a brief research paper on one of the famous families—Fujiwara, Minamoto, or Taira—basing the topic on what can be found in the Reading Selection.

Research Project (B): The Arts of Premodern Japan

Objective: To have students develop an appreciation of the traditional art forms.

Have the students do a brief research paper on one of the traditional art forms from the Kamakura and Ashikaga periods—the tea ceremony, flower arranging, picture scrolls, or Noh drama, for example.

Research Project (C): Literature

Objective: To have students become more familiar with some of Japan's early literary masterpieces, such as the *Heike monogatari* or the *Genji monogatari.*

To each student, assign a section of one of the early epic tales, for memorization of the basic content and presentation before the class. (Note: This can be an exercise in the traditional art form of presenting literature in a formal recitation.)

LESSON 8 Guns and the Unification of the Whole Country

I. KEY POINTS

A. *Grammar Notes*

1. (1) *Ni nagare tsukimashita* ("drifting to"), a compound word (here consisting of *nagareru* and *tsuku*) preceded by the particle *ni* after a place word.

2. (2) *Saseru,* the causative form of the verb *suru,* meaning "to make (someone) do (something)."

B. *Vocabulary*

C. *The Introduction of Guns into Japan*

D. *The Introduction of Christianity*

II. ADDITIONAL INFORMATION

Gairaigo

The Japanese, anxious to introduce Western culture and technology into Japan, began to import many words of American and European origin after the Meiji Restoration in 1868. Since then, a great number of *gairaigo,* or foreign loan words, which are generally written in katakana phonetic script, have come to play an important role in the Japanese language today.

The majority of loan words are of English origin—but they are not necessarily comprehensible to native speakers of English in their Japanized forms. Some examples are: *wan-man kaa* ("one-man car" —a bus with a driver but no conductor), *fain puree* (fine play), *-kyastaa* (newscaster, preceded by a person's name), *kuraimakkusu* (climax), *rajio* (radio), and *yuuhoo* (UFO). Other loan words are of non-English derivation and come mostly from Dutch and Portuguese, since the Netherlands and Portugal were the countries most active in the early opening of Japan to the West, and from France and Germany, from which Japan learned much about medicine, law, and military organization. Some examples of non-English loan words are: *arubaito* (from the German *arbeit,* "side job"), *buriki* (from the Dutch "tin"), and *pan* ("bread" in Portuguese).

Many commonly used foreign loan words are Japanized as follows:

1. By abbreviating the foreign word, as in *depaato* (department store), *apaato* (apartment), *paato* (part-time work), *baito* (side job), *suupaa* (supermarket), *waapuro* (word processor), *biru* (building), *kombi* (combination—speaking of people), *pasokon* (personal computer), and *furasuto* (frustration).

2. By changing the meaning or the usage, as in *manshon* ("mansion"—a high-class apartment or condominium), *reji* ("register"—a cashier), *dema* ("demagogue"—a false rumor), *sumaato* ("smart"—stylish, having a good figure), and *kanningu suru* ("cunning"—cheating in an exam).

3. By adding Japanese suffixes to foreign words, as in *sabo-ru* ("sabotage"—to cut class, play truant), *nau-na* and *nau-ii* ("now"—used to describe something very new in style or fashion), and *atto hoomu-na* ("at home"—to be relaxed and at ease).

4. By combining two loan words or a loan word and a Japanese word, as in *mai hoomu* ("my home"—home that I own), *mai kaa* ("my car"—car that I own), *gasorin sutando* ("gasoline stand"—service station), *OL* or *ooeru* ("office lady"—female office worker), *sarariiman* ("salary man"—company employee), *oorudo misu* ("old miss"—old maid), *dainingu kichin* ("dining kitchen"—combination dining room and kitchen), *kanzume* ("can-packed"—canned food,

with *zume* from *tsumeru*), *denshi renji* ("electronic range"—microwave oven), *kooshuu toire* ("public toilet"), *juutaku roon* ("residence loan"—home loan), *roojin hoomu* ("old-person's home"—nursing home), and *aruchuu* ("alchohol poison"—alcoholic, with *chuu* from *chuudoku,* poison).

In the Japanization of English words, plurals are pronounced in the singular form; and both "r" and "l" are pronounced with an "r" sound. Examples include *sangurasu* for "sunglasses," *raisu* for "rice," and *miruku* for "milk."

One advantage of using loan words is that they can be used to distinguish between something that is Japanese and something foreign. For example: *hirumeshi* (noon rice) is lunch of Japanese food, and *ranchi* (lunch) is a Western-style noon meal; *ryokan* is a Japanese-style inn, and *hoteru* is a foreign-style hotel.

ACTIVITY 1

Sentence Completion

Objective: To check reading comprehension.

Procedure:

1. Prepare a handout based on the Reading Selections, consisting of a paragraph or paragraphs with blanks where items have been omitted.
2. Have students read the passage provided and fill in the blanks with an appropriate response.
3. At the end of an allotted time limit (e.g., twenty minutes), collect papers.

ACTIVITY 2

Listening Comprehension

Objective: To give students practice in understanding what is said out loud and reproducing what is said, in writing.

Procedure:

1. Hand out to the students a written passage, with blanks in place of certain words or phrases, to be read aloud by the teacher.
2. Have the students fill in the blanks after the passage has been read.
3. Collect the handouts, and check and grade them.

ACTIVITY 3

Reading Comprehension

Objective: To check reading comprehension.

Procedure:

1. Hand out reading material, with questions included.
2. Have the students read the material silently.
3. Have the students answer the questions.
4. Collect the handouts, and check and grade them.

ACTIVITY 4

Gairaigo (Borrowed Words)

Objective: To help students recognize borrowed words in newspapers and other publications.

Materials: Newspapers, magazines, or other Japanese-language publications.

Procedure:

1. Divide students into two teams.
2. Using Japanese-language publications, have the teams make lists of as many borrowed words as possible, within a certain time limit.
3. After each team has made a list, have one team try to stump the other by asking for (a) the pronunciation and (b) the meaning of each item on the list.

Note: An increasing number of words and expressions is passing from various languages into Japanese, of which English items constitute the vast majority. But the meaning, nuance, and pronunciation may differ from the original language, so it can be fun to collect and study some of these new words.

Examples:

Japanese	*English*
チャーミング	charming
コントロール	control
デラックス	deluxe
フロント	front (hotel registration counter)
ギブアンドテイク	give and take
ハンデーキャップ	handicap
ハイパワー	high-power
インスタント	instant
レジャー	leisure
マイナス	minus
モデル	model
モーニング・セット	morning set
ストアー	store
ストライク	strike
スタイル	style
ユニーク	unique

LESSON 9 The Edo Period (A): Isolationism and the Social System

I. KEY POINTS

A. *Grammar Notes*

1. (1) *Katta* and its antonym *maketa* preceded by *ni.*
2. (2) *Made,* used to show that something is an example of an extreme situation, and replacing the particles *ga* and *o.*
3. (4) *Koto ni natte iru,* meaning that something has already been decided (by agreement or rule).

B. *Vocabulary*

C. *The Period of National Isolation*

II. ADDITIONAL INFORMATION

Christianity

In 1549, Christianity was introduced into Japan with the landing of the Jesuit missionary Francis Xavier at Kagoshima. Jesuit priests, who often accompanied Portuguese traders to Japan, engaged in missionary activities and spread the gospel. The number of converts to Christianity grew rapidly in the first few decades after its introduction, especially in Kyushu and some southwestern provinces. (Some sources give the number of Christian converts as 200,000, while others say it was as high as 500,000).

Hideyoshi, the military leader of Japan at the end of the sixteenth century, grew fearful of Christianity. He and early Tokugawa leaders saw Christianity as a threat to the political stability that they had fought so hard to establish. They felt that Christianity, which stressed loyalty to God and prohibited the killing of fellow human beings, would undermine feudal authority, which was based on loyalty to the lord and a willingness to kill to gain power and territory for him.

As a result, all foreign missionaries were expelled and Japanese Christians mercilessly persecuted. By 1638, Christianity had all but been eradicated from feudal Japan. It was not until after the Meiji Restoration in 1873 that the prohibition against Christianity was lifted.

The Period of National Isolation

Japan enjoyed over 250 years of peace under the uninterrupted rule of the Tokugawa family (1603–1867). During this period, the government strictly controlled the political, economic, and even personal activities of the Japanese people. Any threat to feudal authority was promptly, and often ruthlessly, stamped out. Thus, Christianity, viewed as a highly malignant menace by the government, was ordered eradicated. By 1638, the authorities had succeeded in virtually eliminating it. To ensure that Christianity and other "dangerous" foreign beliefs would never again threaten their political stability and internal security, the Tokugawas implemented a policy of isolation from the outside world. For over two hundred years thereafter, from 1638 to 1853, Japan virtually closed its doors to the rest of the world.

Under the seclusion policy, Christianity and the foreign trade that accompanied it were prohibited (the Dutch and Chinese, however, were excluded from this ban and were allowed to land at Nagasaki in Kyushu; some trade with the Koreans also continued). Travel by Japanese to foreign countries was also strictly forbidden. Moreover, from 1636, Japanese who were overseas were banned from returning to their homeland. The government wanted no foreign ideas introduced into Japan for the sake of internal peace and security.

Two hundred years of isolation from the rest of the world had a great impact on Japan. It strengthened Japan's sense of national identity, but also placed a veil of mystery over the country. The government-imposed seclusion was also responsible for Japan's technological retardation during a time in which the Western world was blossoming with new innovations and advances in technology.

ACTIVITY 1

Kanji Review

Objective: To review individual kanji and kanji compounds.

Materials: Cards for writing kanji.

Procedure:

1. Write kanji compounds on cards. Snip the cards in half so that there is one kanji to a card.
2. Have the students rearrange the cut cards to see how many different compound words they can make from the individual kanji.
3. The student making the largest number of compound words wins.

Variation: This activity may be played as a game by having two or more students compete.

ACTIVITY 2

Sentence Scramble

Objective: To review sentence structure.

Procedure:

1. Have columns of scrambled sentences ready on the chalkboard, five sentences to a column.
2. Divide the class into as many teams as there are columns of sentences.
3. Assign each team to a column, with the objective of indicating the proper sequence of the sentences.
4. The first team to finish ordering the sentences properly wins.

ACTIVITY 3

Constructing Complex Sentences

Objective: To enable the student to combine two simple sentences into one complex sentence.

Procedure:

1. Explain what a complex sentence is.
2. Using the following example, go over the construction of a complex sentence.

   Ex. a. 職人はものを作る人です。
   b. 商人はものを売買する人です。

   職人はものを作る人で、商人はものを売買する人です。

3. Have prepared in advance several pairs of simple sentences; present these to the students and have them combine each pair into a complex sentence.

Sample sentences:

1. a. それぞれの身分は生まれた時からきまっていました。
   b. 自分の意志で職業や住む所を変えることはできませんでした。

   それぞれの身分は生まれた時からきまっていて、自分の意志で職業や住む所を変えることはできませんでした。

2. a. 百姓は自分の大名から田畑をもらって米を作りました。
   b. (百姓は) 大体、しゅうかくの半分を税として大名におさめなければなりませんでした。

   百姓は自分の大名から田畑をもらって米を作り、大体、しゅうかくの半分を税として大名におさめなければなりませんでした。

3. a. さむらいは百姓からとりたてた米を食べていました。
   b. また、(さむらいは) それを市場で金にかえて生活していました。

   さむらいは百姓からとりたてた米を食べ、また、それを市場で金にかえて生活していました。

ACTIVITY 4

Human Monopoly Game

Objective: General practice and review.

Materials: Cardboard, white utility paper, markers, scissors, glue.

Procedure:

1. Before the activity, construct a large die/pair of dice (using Japanese numbers would be very effective).
2. In class, arrange the desks as if they were "squares" on a game board.
3. Divide the class into two teams.
4. Roll the die/dice to determine how many seats ("squares" or "spaces") the first player from the first team will be allowed to move.
5. From among several categories of questions (having to do with kanji, hiragana, katakana, translation, etc.) choose a question to ask each player in turn. If a player gets the question right, he or she gets to move the number of seats designated by the throw of the die/dice. If students happen to end up at the same seat, they just "pile up." Some seats will be marked with an "X"—which means that whoever lands there must return "home."
6. Award points for each member who reaches the last seat (the "home" or "goal").

Variation: Using the same concept and rules, this activity could be carried out by moving objects on a large game board (which can be created in advance). Although this may not involve as much physical activity, the game board could be filled with many Japanese things, including pictures and writing. As in any other game, individual participation is as important as team effort.

LESSON 10 The Edo Period (B): Learning, Industry, and the Culture of the Townspeople

I. KEY POINTS

A. *Grammar Notes*

1. (1) *Hiromeru* versus *hiromaru:* examples of two different verb forms derived from the same root.
2. (2) *Na* after an adjectival nominal, and *no* after a nominal sometimes omitted.

B. *Vocabulary*

C. *The Revolution in Industry and Culture*

II. ADDITIONAL INFORMATION

Confucianism

Confucianism was introduced into Japan between the sixth and ninth centuries. It was overshadowed by Buddhism, however, until the establishment of the Tokugawa regime in the seventeenth century. The shogunate viewed the Confucian ideals of loyalty to the ruler, filial piety, and morality as useful tools for maintaining feudal authority. The samurai had become a literate class, and many began to study carefully the Confucian doctrines and classics. Confucianism also had a great impact on the status of women in Japan. Coming from male-dominated China, Confucianism relegated women to subordinate roles and curtailed their freedom. Women, it was asserted, basically existed for the purpose of having children and perpetuating the family line.

Although many Confucian ethical beliefs were seen as convenient devices for maintaining the authority of the Tokugawa family, other values conflicted with the feudal system of government. Confucian philosophy advocated that men of superior intellect, education, and morality should rule. This, however, conflicted with the Tokugawa system of choosing leaders through family lineage. Those directly descended from the Tokugawa were the ones who ruled, usually regardless of their capabilities or qualifications. By the nineteenth century, however, some samurai began to argue that greater leadership responsibilities should be given to more competent men.

Confucian ideals continue to exert considerable influence upon the Japanese today. The great emphasis placed upon education, hard work, and loyalty by modern Japanese, for example, can be traced to the Confucian values introduced hundreds of years ago.

Terakoya

Terakoya was the system of schooling started in the Buddhist temples. The curriculum consisted mostly of reading and writing Chinese characters, as well as abacus training in the more commercial districts. In the late feudal period, this system spread throughout Japan, raising the standard of education.

Ukiyoe

Ukiyoe literally means "pictures of the floating world." This type of painting and wood-block printing started in the seventeenth century and continued through the nineteenth century in Japan. The paintings usually depicted the pleasure quarters, women, and landscapes. Ando Hiroshige is considered one of the great artists of the *ukiyoe* genre and is known especially for his "Fifty-three Views of the Tokaido Highway" series. Other famous artists were Katsushika Hokusai, noted for his prints of Mount Fuji; Kitagawa Utamaro for his beautiful women; and Toshusai Sharaku for his Kabuki actors.

Kabuki

Kabuki is a traditional Japanese popular play with singing and dancing, originated by a woman dancer, Izumo-no-Ookuni, in the seventeenth century. However, since women were prohibited from acting in public by the Tokugawa Shogunate, Kabuki was performed by males exclusively. Thus the women's roles in Kabuki were played by male actors. Shamisen playing, singing, and flute music from Noh and folk theater were used in Kabuki drama and dancing.

Haiku

Haiku is a short poetic form consisting of three lines of five, seven, and five syllables, which developed during the seventeenth century. Although terse and somewhat restricted in form, the haiku is highly suggestive and evocative. As a popular form of self-expression, haiku were often inspired by experiences with or insights into nature and life. The haiku is still a favorite among many Japanese today, and it is also gaining recognition and popularity among Westerners.

Basho

Matsuo Basho (1644–1694) or simply Basho, was a master of the haiku. Recognized as the greatest of all haiku poets, Basho was able to transform a mere seventeen syllables into beautiful, refined, and powerfully suggestive verse. Basho strived for freshness in his poems and was responsible for introducing originality into the imagery of haiku.

Saikaku

Ihara Saikaku (1642–1693), popularly known in literary circles merely as Saikaku, is said to be the greatest fiction writer and novelist of the Tokugawa period. Unlike Lady Murasaki, who depicted the lives of the aristocracy in her monumental *Tale of Genji,* Saikaku often drew the ideas for his characters from the merchant class and the commoner townspeople. Noted for his ability to reveal the essence of human nature, Saikaku wrote realistic works that often offered piercing insights into the society of that era.

Chikamatsu Monzaemon

Chikamatsu Monzaemon (1653–1724), a magnificent dramatist of the Edo period, is often regarded as the greatest playwright Japan has ever produced. He wrote most of his plays for the *jooruri* or puppet theater. Many of them, however, were later adapted for Kabuki. While Chikamatsu wrote historical plays about warriors in battle, he also wrote about the tragic experiences of common people—merchants, prostitutes, store clerks. Many of his works were based on incidents occurring in his own contemporary society.

ACTIVITY I

Bingo

Objective: Visual and aural comprehension—to have students practice learned vocabulary through seeing and hearing.

Materials: "Bingo" sheets with newly learned kanji written on them, a box, and kanji flash cards.

Procedure:

1. Announce that there will be no discussion and no writing anything down.
2. Pass out the bingo sheets with the newly learned kanji on them.
3. From a box containing cards with kanji identical to what is on the bingo sheets, pick out a kanji and say it aloud.

4. Have the students identify the identical kanji on their sheets and mark them.
5. When a player has all the squares covered, calls out "bingo," and reads back all the kanji correctly, then that player wins.

Variation: Instead of kanji, use recent vocabulary.

ACTIVITY 2

Kanji Review

Objective: To give students more practice in kanji writing and comprehension.

Procedure:

1. Before the activity, identify kanji from previous chapters that students seem to have difficulty learning.
2. In class, call out the kanji, and have students write the kanji along with their meanings.
3. Have students write a sentence with each kanji.

ACTIVITY 3

Making Games

Objective: To develop interesting new activities.

Procedure:

1. Divide the class (ideally about thirty students) into groups of five each.
2. Have each group come up with a game for practicing or reviewing what they have learned (it may be an adaptation of a game that they already know).
3. Have the games performed in class, and make sure that everyone participates.

ACTIVITY 4

Football

Objective: To review and reinforce kanji and vocabulary already learned.

Materials: Large piece of paper (or poster board), marker, kanji flash cards.

Procedure:

1. On a large piece of paper, draw a football field, with sections to represent ten-yard intervals. Place a paper or cardboard football on the fifty-yard line.
2. Divide the class into two teams.
3. Hold up a kanji card and ask the first player on the first team to read the kanji. If the kanji is read correctly, the football advances ten yards, and the student has another chance. The football is advanced ten yards for every correct answer. When the football reaches the goal line, six points are awarded—and if one additional correct answer is given, the team receives an "extra point."

4. If the student answers incorrectly before the ball reaches the goal, then it is a "fumble"—and the other team takes over.

Variation: This game may be played by two teams or by two individuals. In addition to the reading, the student may be required to give the meaning of the kanji in English. Or vocabulary items may be substituted for kanji, or the students may be asked to make a sentence with kanji or vocabulary.

LESSON 11 The Meiji Period Following the Meiji Restoration

I. KEY POINTS

A. *Grammar Notes*

1. (1) *Ni kaesu,* meaning "to give back to," preceded by the particle *ni* after a person or place to whom or to which something is returned.

B. *Vocabulary*

C. *The Meiji Restoration*

II. ADDITIONAL INFORMATION

Fukuzawa Yukichi

Fukuzawa Yukichi (1835–1901) was an intellectual born of the samurai class in Kyushu. An advocate of Westernization, he was responsible for spreading and popularizing knowledge of the West during the 1860s and 1870s. Eclectic in his approach to philosophy, Fukuzawa drew from various sources and was influenced by concepts such as those put forth by social Darwinists and Rousseau. Also an ardent advocate of the freedom and equality of man, Fukuzawa founded the first school based on modern ideas and Western principles in 1858 (ten years before the Meiji Restoration). Named Keio Gijuku after the Keio era in which it was founded, it is today the oldest and one of the most prestigious private schools in Japan.

Even today, Fukuzawa is so highly respected that his picture appears on the new 10,000-yen bills.

Natsume Soseki

Natsume Soseki, whose real name was Natsume Kinnosuke (1867–1916), is often regarded as the greatest novelist of the Meiji era. After graduating from the prestigious Tokyo Imperial University with a degree in English literature, Soseki went on to London University on a scholarship provided by the Japanese Ministry of Education. There he studied for about three years and read profusely in a broad range of subjects. He then returned to Tokyo and taught English literature at Tokyo Imperial University.

In 1905 Soseki began his career as a writer. Given his background in English literature, it is not surprising that his early works were influenced by English novels. However, well-versed in Chinese and Japanese as well as in English literature, Soseki later combined elements of both Eastern and Western literary traditions in many of his works. He was a writer of great originality, but dealt primarily with the daily experiences and private lives of ordinary people, particularly the middle class. Through his literary creations, Soseki often made comments, observations, and criticisms of Japanese society.

Among his most famous works are *Kokoro* (The Heart of Things), *Wagahai wa neko de aru* (I Am a Cat), and *Botchan.*

Mori Ogai

Although Mori Ogai (1862–1922) is known as one of the leading writers of early twentieth-century Japan, he was actually trained as a medical doctor and led a dual career as both doctor and writer.

Like many bright, ambitious young men of the Meiji era, Ogai, after his graduation from Tokyo University Medical School, went abroad to study. He spent several years in Germany. This episode in his life apparently had considerable influence on Ogai, as many of his experiences as a young man in Europe are found interspersed in his writings.

As a contemporary of Natsume Soseki, he is often contrasted with the latter. Soseki was quite liberal, compared to Ogai, who was known for his rigid, almost samurai-like values. It has been said that Ogai attempted to revive the high ethical and moral standards of the samurai in his literary works.

ACTIVITY 1

Kanji Game

Objective: To review kanji by making kanji compounds.

Materials: Cards for writing kanji.

Procedure:

1. Prepare kanji cards (make enough sets of cards to go around the class).
2. Before the game, review all of the kanji on the cards.
3. Divide the class into small groups and pass out the kanji cards.
4. Have each group form compounds with the individual kanji.
5. The team with the most compounds wins.

Example kanji:

産　近　農　新　職　業
維　政　京　治　大　東
聞　首　生　校　代　明
中　文　時　小　都　学

ACTIVITY 2

Concentration Game

Objective: To review the Reading Selection.

Materials: Rectangular cards.

Procedure:

1. On separate cards, write the noun and verb phrases found in the list below.
2. Mix the cards and let the students connect the right noun phrases with the right verb phrases.
3. This can be either an individual or a team activity.

Noun and Verb Phrases:

1. 自由と平等を人々に	1. 教えました。
2. 西洋の国々との貿易が	2. 始まりました。
3. 世の中が	3. 変わりました。
4. 幕府を	4. たおしました。
5. 東京が日本の首都に	5. なりました。
6. 身分制度が	6. はいしされました。
7. 人々は自分の意志で職業を	7. えらぶことができるようになりました。
8. 産業が	8. 発達しました。
9. えらい人もたくさん	9. でました。

10.	西洋の歌が	10.	紹介されました。
11.	牛肉を	11.	食べるようになりました。
12.	くつを	12.	はきました。
13.	ちょんまげを	13.	落しました。
14.	権力を天皇に	14.	返しました。
15.	社会や人々の生活のようすをえがいた作品は	15.	今でも広く読まれています。

ACTIVITY 3

Question and Answer Game

Objective: To practice listening and reading.

Materials: Slips of paper, a box.

Procedure:

1. Carefully review the Reading Selection and its accompanying question-answer drill (see Lesson 11 in the textbook). Copy each question on a separate slip of paper. Place the slips in a large envelope or in a box.
2. Divide the class into two groups or into groups of four or five students each.
3. Pull out a slip of paper and read the question on it, repeating the question if necessary.
4. Ask the students to skim through the Reading Selection in their textbook for the correct answer. The answer must be in Japanese.
5. Award a point for each correct answer. The team with the most points wins.

LESSON 12 Modern Times

I. KEY POINTS

A. *Grammar Notes*

1. (1) *Ni hantai suru,* meaning "to oppose" or "to object," in which *hantai suru* is preceded by the particle *ni* after the expression indicating what is being opposed.

2. (2) *Aruki dasu,* meaning "begin walking," where the compound verb consists of the stem of the *-masu* form of the verb + *dasu,* meaning "begin . . . -ing" or "start . . . -ing."

B. *Vocabulary*

C. *World War II*

II. ADDITIONAL INFORMATION

The Sino-Japanese War

After a rapid period of modernization and economic growth in the Meiji period, Japan began to flex its military muscle. From 1894 to 1895, Japan fought with China over the control of Korea, which was of great strategic importance to both countries. After defeating its giant neighbor with surprising ease, Japan gained many concessions as its spoils of war. As a result of being defeated, China had to relinquish Taiwan, the Pescadores Islands, and southern Manchuria to Japanese control, and all Chinese influence was removed form Korea. In addition, Japan was paid a large indemnity and given the same diplomatic and trading privileges as those that had been acquired by the major Western powers. Japan, however, was forced to return southern Manchuria to China through the pressure of a coalition formed by Russia, France, and Germany. But with its victory over China, Japan's confidence in its military strength grew, and the stage was set for future confrontations with the other major powers.

The Russo-Japanese War

Having handily defeated China in 1895, Japan took on Russia in another war, in 1904. The objective of this next conflict, as with the Sino-Japanese War, was control over Korea. Russia, which along with Germany and France had forced the Japanese to return southern Manchuria to the Chinese in 1895, claimed southern Manchuria for itself just three years later. As a result, Russia became the dominant force in Manchuria. The next step for the Russians was the control of Korea. Sensing the threat, Japan formed an alliance with Britain, prepared to neutralize Russian naval forces in East Asia, and then declared war on Russia. The Japanese Navy then proceeded to destroy Russia's European fleet in the Sea of Japan. Although far stronger than Japan, Russia was forced to fight a war in one of the most remote and least accessible regions of its empire, and was soundly defeated.

Japan was again richly rewarded for its victory. With Russia's defeat, Korea virtually came under Japanese domination. Japan also acquired the southern part of Manchuria and half of the railways that Russia had established in Manchuria. Rather than paying Japan as indemnity, Russia relinquished to the Japanese the southern half of the Sakhalin Island, strategically located just north of Hokkaido.

Japan's decisive victory over Russia not only allowed Japan to expand its colonial empire but also signified its emergence as a new world power.

The Annexation of Korea

By battling and defeating both China and Russia, Japan had its path cleared for the annexation of Korea in 1910. The Japanese modernized and brought about the economic development of Korea. Among other things they introduced new communication, education, and transportation systems. On the other hand, however, Korea was exploited and its people subjugated by an oppressively efficient colonial government. The detested Japanese domination over Korea finally came to an end with Japan's surrender at the end of World War II.

Kawabata Yasunari

Kawabata Yasunari (1899–1972), recognized as one of the finest Japanese writers of the twentieth century, won world-wide acclaim with his award-winning novel *Snow Country.* Said to be Kawabata's best work, *Snow Country* won the Nobel Prize for Literature in 1968. Kawabata thus became the first Japanese and only the second Asian to win that prestigious award.

Kawabata has been described as a more traditional writer who belonged to the "Neo-Sensationalist" school. As a representative of his school, he opposed the overuse of graphic realism and emphasized instead an indirect sensuality. Edward Seidensticker, who translated *Snow Country* and other works by the great writer, has said that Kawabata wrote in a "haiku manner." That is, he incorporated many qualities of the haiku into his novels.

Kawabata was also known for his ability to paint revealing psychological portraits of women. A somber tone pervades much of his work, as Kawabata often wrote of loneliness and "wasted beauty."

Kawabata Yasunari committed suicide in 1972.

The Occupation of Japan (1945–1951)

The occupation of Japan was led by General Douglas MacArthur. Although his official title was Supreme Commander for the Allied Powers, his orders for the execution of policy came directly from the United States Government; policy was set by the American Government, to be approved by the Far Eastern Commission in Washington. The Far Eastern Commission comprised those nations who had fought against Japan.

The three major changes that occurred as the result of the occupation were the demilitarization, the democratization, and the rehabilitation of Japan.

The occupation years are looked upon by some as marking the final break from the past and the acceptance by Japan of institutions and values not influenced by feudal or Confucian tradition.

ACTIVITY 1

Twenty Questions

Objective: To give students an opportunity to express themselves using the vocabulary and structure that they have learned; to enable students to ask questions in Japanese about the aspects of Japanese history covered in the lessons.

Procedure:

1. Divide the class into several groups.
2. Have the first group think of something and tell the class whether it is a person, place, or thing. (The teacher may make suggestions.)
3. Have the other groups take turns asking questions (not more than twenty) to try and guess the answer.

徳川時代ですか。	はい。
有名な人ですか。	いいえ。
町ですか。	はい。
江戸ですか。	はい，江戸です！

4. Award points to the group that guesses the correct answer or makes the most use of Japanese during the game.

ACTIVITY 2

Describing an Object

Objective: To provide students with writing and listening comprehension practice.

Procedure:

1. Have each student prepare six written statements about some object in the classroom. (When students become proficient at this, vocabulary items from the lessons in the text may be used; for example: Hiroshima, *genshi bakudan, danjo byoodoo,* Kawabata Yasunari.)
2. Have Student A describe an object, and Student B guess what is being described.
3. If Student B guesses correctly, then have Student B describe an object to another student. If a correct answer is not given, then have student B read the next sentence of his or her description, and so on.
4. Have the guessing continue until all six statements have been read.
5. If no one has guessed the object by the end of the sixth question, then give the answer.

ACTIVITY 3

Sentence Race

Objective: To practice constructing sentences.

Procedure:

1. Divide the class into two or more teams.
2. Have the first player on each team go to the board and write a simple sentence about modern times in Japan.
3. Have each member of the respective teams in turn add a word or phrase to that team's sentence. (Each additional word or phrase must contribute new information. Set a time limit.)
4. Award a point to the team that completes an intelligible sentence in which each team member has participated.
5. Repeat the procedure. The team with the most points wins.

LESSON 13 The Constitution of Japan and Democratic Government

I. KEY POINTS

A. *Grammar Notes*

1. (1) The particle *ni* used with *motozuite* and *shitagatte.*
2. (3) *Koto* used as a nominal referring to the subject of the previous clause.
3. (6) *Kara natte iru,* meaning "consists of."
4. (7) The prefix *kaku,* meaning "each."

B. *Vocabulary*

C. *The Constitution of Japan*

II. ADDITIONAL INFORMATION

The Diplomacy of Peace

The end of World War II marked the beginning of Japan as a peace-loving, democratic nation with its people committed to promoting world peace. The Constitution of 1946 declared that the Japanese people would renounce war forever and work toward settling international disputes through dialogue and international cooperation. With this ideal expressed in peaceful diplomacy, Japan believes that its security and well-being will be maintained.

To implement this diplomacy of peace, Japan has been participating in the activities of the United Nations and promoting the peaceful settlement of international disputes and the strengthening of the rules of international law. Japan serves on the Security Council, the Economic and Social Council, and other councils and boards of the United Nations.

Japan and the United States enjoy a close and firm relationship that is the cornerstone of Japan's foreign policy.

To promote mutual understanding and friendship with all countries, Japan established the Japan Foundation in 1972, its purpose being to facilitate a cultural exchange that will enrich the world community.

The Constitution

The most important political change that came about as a result of the Occupation was the revision of the Japanese Constitution. The new draft appeared in early 1946 and was presented to the Japanese people on March 6, 1947.

A major objective of the new Constitution was to create a representative form of government, in which there would be no single center of authority. As a result, the Emperor became the "symbol of the State," and his actions would be subject to cabinet approval.

There was also a decentralization of the economy and a reform of the education system.

ACTIVITY I

Oral Response Practice

Objective: To test understanding of the lesson and provide practice in oral summarizing.

Procedure:

1. Have the class read aloud each sentence from the first paragraph of the Reading Selection.

2. Call on individual students to give the meaning, in English, of each sentence.
3. Call on one student to give the general meaning, in English, of the entire first paragraph.
4. Call on another student to give the general meaning of the same paragraph, this time in simple Japanese.
5. Repeat the procedure for the remaining paragraphs in the Reading Selection.

Variation: This activity can be either a group effort or an individual written assignment in class or at home. In class, the Japanese responses may be written on the board as the sentences are given.

ACTIVITY 2

Impromptu Oral Question and Answer

Objective: To provide listening and speaking practice.

Procedure:

Ask individual students two or more related questions on the chapter (the oral drill questions in the text may be used here).

ACTIVITY 3

Question and Answer Game

Objective: To provide listening and speaking practice.

Procedure:

1. Divide the class into two teams.
2. Direct a question to a member on one team. The student must try to answer in more than one sentence, to earn the most points for his or her team.
3. Award one point for each correct sentence in the response.

LESSON 14 Industrial Development and Foreign Trade

I. KEY POINTS

A. *Grammar Notes*

1. (1) *Tatta no,* meaning "only," and preceding a quantity word.
2. (2) *De,* meaning "because," following a nominal clause with *koto* and giving the reason for the statement that follows.
3. (3) *Dake dewa,* following a nominal, an adjective, or a verb in the formal form, meaning "not enough."
4. (4) *Hazu,* a nominal with a modifier, meaning that what is stated in the modifier "is expected."
5. (5) *Ni* preceding *doryoku suru* after a nominal or nominal equivalent for which effort is expended.
6. (6) *Ni* + *hokori o motsu,* meaning "takes pride in. . . ."
7. (7) The verb *nai kagiri* making a condition for which the following statement can be true.
8. (8) *Ni kan shite mo,* preceded by a nominal or noun clause with *koto,* meaning "concerning," "about," "on," etc., depending on the context.

B. *Vocabulary*

II. ADDITIONAL INFORMATION

Additional Facts about Japanese Agriculture (1980)

Agriculture has always been an important part of the Japanese economy. By 1980, however, only 13 percent of all households were engaged in farming. Moreover, only 13.4 percent of all such farm households were engaged in agriculture full-time. The other 86.6 percent had additional sources of income.

Agriculture in Japan is primarily a family activity. The farms, by American standards, are small, averaging a little less than 2.5 acres. Yields, however, are high, as intensive farming practices are employed. Machinery and new technology were introduced to compensate for the declining farm labor force.

The main crop produced is rice, the staple of the Japanese diet. Japan is completely self-sufficient in rice production. In 1979, for example, more than 12 million tons were produced. In the same year, Japanese farmers also produced 16.3 million tons of vegetables, which satisfied most of the domestic demand. Japan, however, still lags behind in the production of cereals such as wheat and barley and different types of legumes (for example, peas and beans), and it imports most of these farm products. As far as milk and dairy products are concerned, Japan produces enough to meet 87 percent of its domestic needs.

In the past twenty years, meat production has increased to meet the growing demand. Pork and chicken, in particular, are heavily produced by the Japanese. In 1979, the output of pork and chicken was 1,429,928 and 938,184 tons, respectively. In addition, 401,665 tons of beef and veal as well as 4,308 tons of horsemeat were produced. This, however, was not enough to meet consumer demand, and 791,000 tons of meat also had to be imported.

The Iron and Steel Industry

In spite of the heavy dependence on imported raw materials such as iron ore, coal, and scrap iron, due to its poor mineral resources, Japan ranks as the world's second largest steel-producing nation

(1986). The key to this development has been the modernization of facilities and the new technologies developed in Japan and other countries. The industry has developed high-strength steel, weather-resistant steel, surface-treated steel sheets, and the super-size, wide flange beams, which are being used in the construction of highrise buildings in increasing numbers.

From even before World War II, Japan has been not only self-sufficient, but has exported ships, textiles, and electrical machinery to Asia and other parts of the world. Japanese cars, buses, trucks, and motor supplies are supplied to many continents, and the export of these items in 1984 was over 70 percent of Japan's total exports.

The Fishing Industry

The seas surrounding Japan are rich with marine life, and the Japanese have depended upon them for a major part of their food supply. Hence, Japan has been one of the major fishing nations in the world. In 1980 the total fishing catch was 11,122,000 metric tons, which represented 14.7 percent of the total world fishing catch.

The fishing industry in Japan can be divided into three major categories: coastal, offshore, and deep-ocean fishing. Coastal fishing is done with nets set by boats, or by artificial breeding in shallow waters (that is, fish farming). In recent years the coastal fishing industry has shrunk because of water pollution by waste from the factories along the coast.

Pearls and oysters are cultured in shallow waters, and sea bream, prawns, and scallops are also raised by shallow-water aquaculture methods. Production from aquaculture represents 8.9 percent of the total fisheries production.

Offshore fishing is conducted by smaller vessels, and in 1980 these brought in almost 30 percent of the total value of fisheries production. Deep-ocean fishing involves large vessles that operate in waters far from Japan. In 1980 the deep-ocean catch amounted to over 19 percent of the total catch. Due to the two hundred-mile limits set by various nations, Japan's deep-ocean fishing (for example, for salmon and sea trout) has been hit hard, especially in the northern Pacific. Therefore Japan has been shifting away from fishing to sea farming to develop new marine resources. The focus is on catching fish within its own 200-mile zone, by sea-farming and coastal and off-shore fishing. Japan has implemented various measures to regulate the major fisheries, carrying out artificial hatching and stocking of fish and shellfish. Whaling is still practiced by Japan.

Tsukiji

The Tokyo Metropolitan Central Wholesale Market, better known as Tsukiji, conducts wholesale transactions in fish, meat, eggs, vegetables, and fruits, in all forms—fresh, frozen, processed, dried, etc. It dates from 1932, and is one of the largest of its kind in the world.

From about 4:30 A.M. the day begins, every day except Sunday, inside the fan-shaped wholesale sheds where skilled dealers check the day's catch to decide what prices to bid when the auction begins at five A.M. Nearly forty thousand vehicles visit the market each day—a scene without equal anywhere else in the world.

There are some six hundred different species of edible fish in Japanese waters, but Tsukiji deals with only one hundred or so of them. Other fish are brought in from as far as New Zealand and the Bering Sea. Of these, tuna is the most valuable per pound, and accounts for about 10 percent of trading at Tsukiji. Over 90 percent of the seafood as well as most of the vegetables consumed in Tokyo, valued at a wholesale price of ten million dollars per day, are supplied by Tsukiji.

Over seventy thousand persons are involved daily in the activity at Tsukiji, and only a few (mostly tourists) are without credentials. Those with credentials are the wholesalers, licensed by the Minister of Fisheries and Agriculture, who hire auctioneers to sell the catch to dealers, who are licensed by the Governor of Metropolitan Tokyo and who in turn sell to the buyers, who call at the stalls that the dealers operate in the market. The buyers include representatives of restaurants, hotels, and food processors. Tsukiji is well worth at least one visit.

Foreign Trade

Japan today is a major trading country, and a "full-fledged partner in a growing world economy." The Japanese economy depends upon the free flow of international trade. Its major imports are raw materials, such as raw cotton, raw wool, and bauxite; iron ore; crude oil and petroleum; and foodstuffs. The major exports are machinery, equipment, and motor vehicles.

Japan's changing industrial structure and the new trade patterns abroad in recent years have resulted in a shift in the substance and the distribution of the country's foreign trade. Before the war, textile raw materials accounted for over 30 percent of the total imports and more than half of the total exports. In the mid-1980s, this has changed: there has been a sharp rise in the imports of petroleum, iron ore, and non-ferrous metals, reflecting the growing importance of Japan's heavy industries. Meanwhile, exports of metal products, machinery, and chemicals, which used to be about 16 percent, have risen to 86 percent. Automobiles, in particular, have overtaken steel as the top export industry, while shipbuilding has been on the decline, indicating changes in economic conditions throughout the world.

In the distribution of Japanese goods, Asia, especially China, India, and Indonesia, provided the biggest outlet before the war. Today, Japan has its largest commerce with North America, especially the United States, which is Japan's largest single trading partner. For the United States, Japan is the second largest customer after Canada.

Since the price of oil spiraled upward, the two-way trade imbalance between Japan and other countries has become serious, and trade disputes have broken out in a number of areas, particularly with the United States and Western Europe.

ACTIVITY 1

Paragraph Scramble

Objective: To review vocabulary, provide reading practice, and strengthen paragraph development skills.

Materials: Access to ditto or photocopy machine, paper to be cut into slips, envelopes, clips.

Procedure:

1. Make multiple copies of paragraph 2 of the Reading Selection.
2. Cut the paragraph on each sheet into its component sentences. Scramble the sentences and clip each set together or place in an envelope.
3. Divide the class into small groups.
4. Give each group an envelope and tell the group members to put the sentences together in a logical sequence (textbooks may not be used).
5. After all the groups are finished, have each group read the paragraphs that they have assembled.
6. Discuss any discrepancies.

ACTIVITY 2

Headlines

Objective: To provide an opportunity to study Japanese periodicals.

Materials: Japanese newspapers and magazines, cellophane tape.

Procedure:

1. Save up a stock of Japanese periodicals, and cut out large, readable headlines.

2. Distribute the headline slips over a table top, in two piles for separate teams. In each pile, cut the headlines in half and scramble the pile.
3. Divide the class into two teams, and assign each team to a pile.
4. Have each team match the separated headlines in its assigned pile (splice the halves with cellophane tape). Set a time limit.
5. The team with the most headlines correctly matched wins.

Variation: Have each member explain an event or incident related to one of the headlines.

ACTIVITY 3

Dictation

Objective: To review and reinforce learned patterns and kanji.

Procedure:

1. Dictate a passage to the class, one sentence at a time, and repeat each sentence twice.
2. Collect papers, and check and grade them.

LESSON 15 School Life

I. KEY POINTS

A. *Grammar Notes*

1. (1) The verb *au* in a compound-verb expression.

2. (2) *Ba . . . hodo,* meaning "the more . . . the more. . . ."

B. *Vocabulary*

C. *The Japanese Educational System*

II. ADDITIONAL INFORMATION

Education in Japan

The state educational system was decentralized as a result of educational reform during the Occupation period. Some major changes that occurred were the introduction of the 6-3-3-4 system, the transferring of power over portions of the curriculum to local school boards, the establishment of the Parent-Teacher Association, and the creation of new prefectural universities. Revisions of the curriculum and textbooks were sponsored by the Occupation, along with the simplification of the written language.

There is a Board of Education, in each prefecture, city, town, and village, which is responsible for the establishment and management of public schools and other public educational institutions. Families with children about to enter elementary school receive notification from their ward or local municipal offices in the middle of December of the preceding year. The schools usually conduct a guidance meeting for the parents in March, followed by the beginning of school in April.

The Japanese school calendar comprises 240 school days, approximately one-third longer than its American counterpart. Education to the Japanese is seen as an ongoing process. In addition to regular school, over one-half of Japanese youths attend supplementary schools *(juku)* during their elementary and/or secondary school years. This is to enable them to pass an entrance exam to a good school of higher learning. The entrance exams are used as the exclusive means for admission to institutions of higher learning. They measure acquired knowledge and the capability of the student to use his innate ability for disciplined study.

It is clear to students that their future depends solely on meritocratic performance as measured by entrance exams. Therefore, the motivation to study must come from within.

Even after the completion of their formal education, many Japanese continue to enroll in a variety of correspondence courses and special study programs as a means of broadening their knowledge.

Number and Types of Schools

According to the Japanese Ministry of Education, in 1985 there were 25,040 elementary schools, 11,121 junior high schools, 5,453 senior high schools, 62 technical colleges, 543 junior colleges, 460 universities, and 2,520 special training schools in Japan. These schools, in turn, are classified as national, public, or private schools. At the elementary and junior high school levels (education is compulsory through junior high school), the public schools overwhelmingly outnumber the national and private schools. At the high school level, the gap between public and private schools decreases. However, public institutions still outnumber private high schools by more than three to one. "National" schools are very rare at the first three levels. Only about 0.4 percent of the total number of elementary, junior high, and senior high schools are under the auspices of the national government. By contrast, over 87 percent of the technical colleges are sponsored and funded by the national government. The public school–private school ratio for grades 1 through 12 reverses itself at the junior college, university, and special-training school levels. For these three types of schools, private institutions greatly outnumber public and national ones. It has been estimated that nearly 80 percent of all Japanese university students are enrolled in private institutions.

Numbers of Students and Teachers

According to the Japanese Ministry of Education (1986), the number of students in elementary, junior high, and high schools in Japan in 1985 numbered 11,096,000, 5,991,000, and 5,178,000, respectively. In the same year, there were 461,000 elementary, 285,000 junior high, and 267,000 high school teachers.

In the junior colleges there were 371,000 students and 17,800 teachers, while the universities registered 1,849,000 students and 112,300 instructors. Kindergarten education has become very popular in recent years, and in 1985 90 percent of first graders had attended kindergarten. In the twenty years from 1960 to 1980, the number more than doubled to 14.9 million students.

Education Expenses (Source: *Statistical Handbook of Japan,* 1982)

In 1982, the central and local governments spent a prodigious 4,864 billion yen on education and culture—approximately 9.8 percent of the total national budget.

In addition to this, Japanese families with children in the public schools spent their own private funds for school expenses.

When costs for private tutors, private music lessons, *juku,* and/or *yobikoo* lessons (see Volume 2, *Teacher's Manual,* Lesson 2), school entrance examination fees, college and university expenses, and so forth are added together, the amount spent by many Japanese parents for their children's education can be quite considerable. Most families, however, will tolerate, and many do not seem to mind, the expense, since education is seen as the key to success in a status-conscious Japanese society.

Textbooks

All Japanese elementary and secondary schools are required by law to use textbooks in the classroom. In addition, all such textbooks must be accredited and authorized by the Ministry of Education. Books are first screened by the Research Council for Textbook Authorization, a group made up of teachers and individuals experienced with textbooks matters. Based upon their recommendations, a list of authorized textbooks is drawn up. Local school boards then select their books from among those accredited by the Ministry of Education. For national or private institutions, principals have the responsibility for choosing textbooks, again from the government-authorized list. Often, however, the same series of textbooks may be used over wide areas, where more than one local board of education operates (this is particularly true for public elementary and junior high schools). Textbooks are provided free to all students during their compulsory education years.

National versus Private Universities

National Universities are public institutions sponsored and funded by the Japanese central government. The oldest of these is Tokyo University, established in 1877. Its name was changed to Tokyo Imperial University in 1886. Other Imperial Universities were later created by the government. Among these were Kyoto (in 1897), Tohoku in Sendai (in 1907), Kyushu in Fukuoka (in 1910), and Hokkaido in Sapporo (in 1918). The term "Imperial" was deleted after the war, but new National Universities were established, and they now continue to play an important role in Japanese higher education.

In 1980, there were ninety-three National Universities and the number is increasing each year. They represent nearly 21 percent of the 446 universities in the country. The overwhelming majority of four-year institutions of higher learning in 1980 were, however, private (over 71 percent). The remaining 7.6 percent were public universities, that is, schools supported by prefectural or municipal governments.

Private universities are self-supporting and must rely mainly on tuition to sustain themselves. Thus, students of private institutions are generally assessed much higher fees than the nominal tuition paid by students of government-supported National Universities. This does not mean, however, that the

National Universities are of inferior quality. They are, on the contrary, the most or among the most prestigious universities in all of Japan.

Tokyo University is by far the highest-ranking Japanese university, followed by the older and/or more specialized National Universities such as Kyoto and Hitotsubashi. Then come Keio and Waseda, the two oldest and most prestigious private universities. These are closely followed by the National Universities founded after the war, which are also highly respected institutions of higher learning. The majority of private universities fall below these universities in terms of esteem. Thus, the most prestigious universities are also the least expensive, while those of mediocre or poor quality are the most expensive.

As a result of cost and prestige factors, many Japanese students strive to get into National Universities, particularly Tokyo University. It is generally accepted that entrance into Japan's number-one university virtually assures one a prestigious job and higher status in life.

ACTIVITY I

Question and Answer Game

Objective: To review the lesson and reinforce what has been learned.

Materials: Slips of paper, a box.

Procedure:

1. Prepare a good number of questions on material from the previous lessons, and write each question on a slip of paper. (Questions may be selected from the list in the oral drills after each lesson.) Each question should be numbered and then folded and put into a box.
2. Divide the class into two teams.
3. Shake the box and empty the slips of paper onto a table top.
4. Have the students from each team take turns picking up one slip at a time and attempt to answer the question on it. If they cannot answer, have them put the folded slip back on the table and take another one. Set a time limit for each team.
5. If a student answers correctly, award five points to his or her team; if the answer is incorrect, award five "minus" points. (Have one student keep score.)
6. The team with the most points wins.

Variation: This game can be played individually rather than by teams. Students may be graded as if this were a quiz.

ACTIVITY 2

Guessing Game

Objective: To have students practice making precise oral descriptions.

Materials: Large colored pictures of scenery, people, or places.

Procedure:

1. Show the students a picture (preferably of people or places in Japan).
2. Tell the students that you have selected a person, place, or thing to be seen in the picture.
3. Have the students guess what it is by asking questions. Students should be encouraged to use descriptive phrases (rather than single adjectives) in their questions.

Ex. Ki no shita ni tatte iru ojisan desu ka?
Akai burausu o kite kuroi sukaato o haite iru onna no ko desu ka?

4. Award a point for each correct guess. Additional points should be awarded for additional information, such as more than one adjective or adverb. This will encourage complex questions.

The student with the most points wins.

ACTIVITY 3

Complete the Headlines

Objective: To provide the students with an opportunity to study Japanese newspapers or magazines.

Materials: Japanese newspapers and magazines.

Procedure:

1. Cut out large, readable headlines from a number of periodicals.
2. Cut the headlines in half and distribute them over a table top. Make two separate piles of cut halves.
3. Divide the class into two teams.
4. Have each team try to match the halves of as many headlines as possible (splice with cellophane tape). For each headline, write one or more sentences related to it.
5. The winning team is the one with the most headlines correctly matched (each with one or more descriptive sentences).

LESSON 16 The Modernization of Lifestyle and the New Life for Women

I. KEY POINTS

A. *Grammar Notes*

1. (2) *Ni okeru,* a nominal modifier, and *ni oite,* a modifier of parts of speech other than the nominal.

2. (3) *Kango* versus *wago.*

B. *Vocabulary*

II. ADDITIONAL INFORMATION

Beddo-taun

Kenkyusha's New Japanese-English Dictionary defines a *beddo-taun* as "a bedroom town (community, suburb); a commuter's town; a dormitory (suburb)." Space in large Japanese cities is scarce, land prices high, and crowding severe. As a result, people have had to search farther and wider for housing. Many Japanese now live in the suburbs of large cities. These areas have essentially become "commuting towns" in the sense that working people and often students must travel long distances to and from the cities.

Spending three to five hours every day commuting between home and work or school is not unusual for many Japanese who live in suburban areas. Such places are appropriately called "bed towns." After all, given the long commuting hours, just about all one has time for at home is sleep.

Chonan (Eldest Son)

In feudal times, the family and its perpetuation were of considerable importance, particularly to prominent members of the warrior and merchant classes. The eldest son or *chonan* played an especially significant role in the family, for it was usually he who inherited the assets of as well as the responsibility for the family.

Although not strictly adhered to, remnants of this system still remain in modern Japan. In many areas, the eldest son is still expected to take over the family farm or business. Even without a farm or business, however, more responsibility is usually delegated to the *chonan* than to his siblings. For example, the care of elderly parents and the family's ancestral tablets generally rests upon the shoulders of the eldest son and his wife. The custom of looking after parents is slowly declining, especially in urban areas where cramped living quarters make it difficult for three generations to live under a single roof. However, the tradition of the *chonan* assuming responsibility for his parents' welfare is prevalent enough to make women think twice about marrying an eldest son!

Social Security and the Elderly

The social security program in Japan is administered by the Ministry of Health and Welfare and its Social Insurance Agency. The local prefectural and municipal governments provide the day-to-day services through their welfare departments. The program is basically a combination of income security, provided through social insurance and public livelihood assistance, and medical care security through health insurance and public welfare, which includes services for the aged, the physically handicapped, and children lacking a normal home life.

Care of the Elderly

The number of elderly persons requiring more than the average social welfare assistance is still small compared to that in Western nations, but it is steadily growing. Lifetime employment, the seniority wage system, and the welfare programs undertaken by companies are quite extensive in scale and variety. Further, the retirement allowances paid by companies play a great part in the old-age security system.

Life insurance in Japan has a thirty-year maturity period in most cases, and at the end of this period a sum equal to the total premium payment plus the interest is paid in a lump sum by way of a fund for old-age security. Private life insurance is also accorded generous tax benefits, and this helps in providing stability to people's lives in Japan.

Keigo

Language plays an important role in status-conscious Japan. The language one uses generally reflects one's position in society relative to that of the listener. One aspect of Japanese that poses many problems for foreign students of the language as well as for the Japanese themselves is the complex system of honorifics or *keigo*.

Keigo can be divided into (1) respect forms *(sonkeigo)* and (2) humble forms *(kenjoogo). Sonkeigo,* which includes forms such as *ossharu* (to say), *nasaru* (to do), and *goran ni naru* (to see), are used when speaking about the actions of a superior. Humble forms such as *ukagau* (to ask), *moosu* (to say), and *mairu* (to go, to come), on the other hand, are used to refer to one's own actions when speaking to someone of higher status.

One reason for the popular Japanese custom of exchanging name cards *(meishi)* is that the cards reveal the status of the givers. In that way, the parties involved can adjust their speech to reflect their relative status.

The Japanese are fairly strict about the proper use of honorific forms. Those who are not able to use them correctly are sometimes criticized, for *keigo* is an integral part of Japanese language and society.

ACTIVITY 1

Glossing of Unfamiliar Words

For Objectives and Procedure, refer to Lesson 5, Activity 2.

Suggested paragraphs:

日本語の特徴

A. 日本語は話す人の年令、性別、職業、地位などによって、ことば使いがちがう。日本の大会社などでは、今でもことば使いについて、なかなかきびしく、地位の上の人や、会社以外の人と話す時はなるべくていねいに話すし、また、反対に地位の上の人が下の人に話す時は命令形を多く使う。たとえば社長がひしょになにか頼む時は、「この仕事をすぐやってくれたまえ。」とか、「これでいいよ。」とか言うが、普通の社員が部長や課長と話す時は、絶対にそんな表現は使わない。「そうしていただけますか。」とか、「今おでかけですか。」などと言う。一般に女性は男性よりていねいである。

B. 日本語には敬語のほかに方言の問題もある。いわゆる共通語である東京のことばも、実は東京の方言なのである。日本語の方言の場合、問題になるのは、英語は地方によってアクセントは違っても、たいてい同じことばを使うが、日本語の場合、ひとつひとつのことば、すなわち単語が違うからである。たとえば東京では「ありがとう」と言うが、大阪では「おおきに」と言う。大阪弁で「かってきた」と言う意味は東京の「かりてきた」である。地方地方で違ったことばを使っていたのでは、ことばが通じないので、明治以後東京弁を共通語にきめて、日本じゅうの学校で教育している。

—*Learn Japanese* Secondary Text, Volume 7B

ACTIVITY 2

Building a Sentence

Objective: To reinforce sentence structure by building a sentence cumulatively.

Procedure:

1. Divide class into teams of ten or fifteen students each.
2. Choose a topic from a recent lesson and ask a team to build a sentence based on the topic.
3. In the first round, have each member of the team add just one word to the sentence under construction. If the sentence requires punctuation, a person may have to use his or her turn to supply a comma or a period (at the end).
4. After a sentence is completed, tell the class that the second round requires a contribution of two words to the sentence that will be constructed. The third will require three words, and so on.
5. A player is eliminated when the word added does not fit or is otherwise unsuitable.
6. The team that first completes the longest sentence within a set time limit wins.

LESSON 17 Traditional Culture in a Modern Society

I. KEY POINTS

A. *Grammar Notes*

1. (1) *Tomo* following a numeral, meaning "all of the numbers mentioned."

B. *Vocabulary*

C. *Japanese Rituals*

D. *Modern Japanese Homes*

II. ADDITIONAL INFORMATION

Traditional Japanese Art and Western Art

Western art forms and traditional Japanese art exist side by side in Japan today, and they sometimes intermingle. As spectators and practitioners the Japanese have a deep interest in artistic developments. Painting and drawing are unusually popular pastimes. In the main cities, art exhibitions are held throughout the year and draw large crowds. The oldest and most impressive annual art show is the Nitten Art Exhibition, and to be selected for this display is one of the nation's highest art honors.

Since the war, there has been international artistic exchange, and many Japanese art works have been shown abroad. Also, a number of exhibitions of foreign works have been held in Japan. The Japanese International Art Exhibition and the International Biennial Exhibition of Prints in Tokyo and Kyoto are well known throughout the world.

The traditional music played on the *shamisen, shakuhachi,* or *koto* still exists alongside the pop music of today. One of the oldest forms of music, *gagaku,* is still preserved at the Imperial court and the Shinto shrines, and is performed publicly from time to time. Moreover, the three-stringed *shamisen,* the *shakuhachi* (a Japanese wind instrument made of bamboo), and the thirteen-stringed *koto* are still used for solos and as accompaniment for Kabuki and Japanese classical dancing. At the same time, Western music is composed, performed, and enjoyed by all. There are some seven major symphony orchestras, about twenty music schools, and many dancing academies for ballet. Every year there is a steady flow of foreign musicians performing in Japan, and Japanese musicians also perform overseas. The preservation and development of classical Japanese music is being cultivated by Ensemble Nipponia, a chamber orchestra with a broad repertoire using all of the Japanese wind, string, and percussion instruments.

The theatrical arts in Japan are unique and full of variety, ranging from the classical Noh drama to popular vaudeville, from the puppet drama handed down through the centuries to wide-screen motion-picture productions. The three major classical Japanese dramatic forms are Noh, Bunraku (puppet drama), and Kabuki. The oldest of these is Noh, a highly stylized drama that has been kept alive by a hereditary line of Noh artists. Bunraku, the puppet drama, is performed regularly at Asahi-za theater in Osaka and the National Theater in Tokyo. Each puppet is an elaborate doll that is half life-size, whose movements are manipulated by three puppeteers. Puppets perform to the accompaniment of *shamisen* music and narration, creating a powerful illusion of human emotions and feelings. The art form has developed a following abroad, and Bunraku troupes have performed in Europe, Australia, China, and the United States.

The most famous Japanese dramatic form is Kabuki, which is performed, even today, exclusively by men. Kabuki preserves the rich tradition of the past and has been enjoyed by many for more than two centuries. A number of new plays have been written by contemporary authors, and in recent years some new moves have been made to modernize Kabuki. This dramatic art is internationally known and has been presented in Europe, China, the U.S.S.R., Australia, and the United States.

Sports

Both modern and traditional sports are popular in Japan. Among the traditional forms, *sumo* (Japanese wrestling), judo, *kendo* (Japanese fencing), and *kyuudoo* (Japanese archery) are especially popular. Judo, which developed from *juujutsu,* is popular today not only in Japan, but in many other countries as well. It was one of the events in the 18th Olympics held in Tokyo. International championships are now held regularly in different areas of the world.

Baseball is one of the most popular sports in Japan. It has been described as the national sport, and any game, whether amateur or professional, attracts a very large crowd. Since 1946 a National Sports Festival is held every year as an integrated meet involving all sports in Japan. It is held in three parts, in the winter, summer, and autumn seasons, and is organized by the Japanese Amateur Sports Association. In this competition, the basic representative unit is the prefecture, and more than 16,000 athletes compete every year.

The Japanese Breakfast

A traditional Japanese breakfast might begin with sour, red pickled plum known as an *umeboshi.* Rice, often sprinkled with *nori* (dried seaweed), is also an essential breakfast dish for most Japanese. And breakfast just would not be breakfast without *misoshiru* (bean-paste soup). Along with these, pickled vegetables or some kind of fish is usually eaten. Some Japanese also enjoy having eggs with their meal. Rather than scrambled or fried, however, many Japanese will whip a raw egg, pour it over hot rice (which supposedly cooks the egg), and eat it sprinkled with *nori.* The classic beverage served with breakfast is green tea.

While many Japanese still enjoy this type of traditional breakfast, the advent of Westernization has brought changes in the typical diet. These days, many younger Japanese opt for a more Western diet consisting of bread and coffee. Eggs, ham, and sausages may also be regular breakfast fare for some.

ACTIVITY I

Cloze Exercise

Objective: To improve reading comprehension skills by calling attention to the use of contextual clues and encouraging the practice of making educated guesses.

Materials: Japanese magazines or books.

Procedure:

1. Select three or four paragraphs or a short article from a magazine or book. The selection should be appropriate to the level of the students; that is, students should be familiar with most of the vocabulary and grammar patterns found in it.
2. In a cloze exercise, words are usually deleted at regular intervals (e.g., every fifth or sixth word). If the passage seems easy for the students, delete every third or fourth word. If it is difficult, leave out every sixth or seventh word. (For variation, rather than deleting words at regular intervals, one may (a) delete all verbs at the end of sentences or (b) delete function words such as particles from the passage.)
3. The first sentence in the passage, however, should not be deleted.
4. This may be done as a class or individual activity. In either case, students should be encouraged to read through the passage and fill in the blanks by using contextual clues and making educated guesses.

ACTIVITY 2

Newspaper Shuffle

Objective: To have students become familiar with the average Japanese newspaper.

Materials: Several complete editions of Japanese-language newspapers (try to obtain as many different kinds of dailies as there are teams participating).

Procedure:

Stage 1

1. Have students make up a false newspaper, drawing on different pages from copies of the papers provided. For instance, the cover-backpage folio may be from a month's previous *Asahi Evening News,* and the inner sports section, society news, and advertisements a mixture from the *Japan Times* and *Mainichi Daily News.*
2. Make as many sets of this kind of newspaper as there are participants or teams.
3. Fold each set properly and distribute to all persons or teams playing.
4. Have the players, at a starting signal, reassemble the original paper with all sections matching the title and date of the cover-backpage folio that they have received. The pages, of course, are scattered among the copies handed out to the players. (This means a wild and noisy reassembling process, all of which must be conducted in Japanese.)
5. The first team to get its newspaper properly reassembled wins.
6. At this point the game may be ended, or a second stage may follow.

Stage 2

1. Prepare a list of captions, sentences, or other copy chosen at random from the newspapers used in Stage 1.
2. Hand out the lists to the team captains. Also at this time, distribute scissors to each team.
3. Have each team scan its reassembled newspaper, find the items corresponding to the list received, and then clip out the entire article, advertisement, or whatever in which this item is found.
4. The first team to assemble all of its clippings wins. Again, team-talk must be entirely in Japanese.

(Note: This game, in either or both stages, demands some preparation in advance, but it is well worth the effort. After handling a newspaper in this manner, the students should become more interested in the make-up, style, and order of features found in a Japanese-language daily.)

Stage 3

1. Hold a discussion on the format and content of a Japanese newspaper.
2. Compare the Japanese format with that of the local English-language daily in your area.

APPENDIXES

TRANSLATIONS OF READING SELECTIONS
RESOURCE MATERIALS ON JAPAN
REFERENCES
ANSWER KEYS TO EXERCISE SHEETS

TRANSLATIONS OF READING SELECTIONS

Lesson 1. Japan and Its Climate

Japan is a country of islands. The northernmost island is Hokkaido. Just south of it is Honshu, the largest of the islands. The second largest is Hokkaido, the third is Kyushu, and the fourth is Shikoku. Besides these four large islands, there are many small islands. The whole of Japan is about the size of California in the U.S.

As for the climate of Japan, the changes in the four seasons are very distinct. March, April, and May are the warm spring months, with various kinds of flowers blooming in succession. The cherry blossoms bloom in April. June, July, and August are the summer months. In June, at the beginning of summer, the rainy season called *"tsuyu"* [begins and] continues for about a month, and when the rainy season is over, it is suddenly hot summer. About the end of August the autumnal breeze begins to blow. September, October, and November are the cool autumn months. Autumn is the harvest season, so rice and other crops are gathered, and various kinds of fruits ripen. Toward the end of autumn, the chrysanthemum blooms. Also, the leaves on the trees turn crimson, and Japanese autumn is a very beautiful season. Soon afterward, when the leaves have fallen, it is already winter.

Lesson 2. Japan before the Advent of Buddhist Culture

During the third and fourth centuries, it was still a primitive period and the people's lives were simple. The people of that time fished in the rivers and at the seashore and farmed. Rice was an important crop.

Nature worship was the religion. People prayed to the wonders and curiosities of Mother Nature, such as huge trees, boulders, rivers, mountains, the heavens, the earth, and the sun. This was the beginning of Shinto. A distinctive feature of Japanese Shinto is polytheism. Thus, each god became a symbol of the strength of Mother Nature. For agriculture it was especially necessary to have earth, water, and sun, and what controlled them was not man but the gods alone. Therefore, people worshipped Mother Nature, the symbol of strength, as a god.

During this period, Japan was nonexistent as a nation. Throughout the Japanese archipelago there were several independent clans, and the people believed that the chiefs of their respective clans were descendants of the gods. These clans fought among themselves. As time passed, a clan in the Yamato area conquered the other clans and gradually became strong and great.

Later, about the end of the sixth century, the leader of the Yamato clan came to be called the emperor. People believed the emperor to be a descendant of Amaterasu Oomikami, the Sun Goddess. And of the many gods, they considered Amaterasu Oomikami to be the most important of all.

From about the end of the third century to about the seventh century, when a chief of a powerful clan or the emperor died, a large grave was constructed. *Haniwa* figures were then buried along with him. A *haniwa* in a human form signified a follower. There were also *haniwa* in the forms of houses and animals. Among the graves, the one for Emperor Nintoku in Osaka is said to be the largest; its length is 486 meters (approximately 1,594 feet) and its width 305 meters (approximately 1,000 feet). The large grave and the great number of *haniwa* indicated the strength of his power.

Lesson 3. The Importing of Chinese Culture

During the period when Japan did not even have a writing system, neighboring China already had a writing system and a high level of civilization.

Shotoku Taishi, who assumed the rulership of Japan toward the end of the sixth century, sent students and envoys to China to study law and the ways of government. By about the end of the sixth century, kanji and Buddhism had arrived in Japan.

Today, there are a great many temples and shrines in Nara and Kyoto. Among them, the temple called

Horyuji in Nara is famous as the oldest wooden structure in the world, and it is said to have been built by Shotoku Taishi to propagate Buddhism.

The approximately one hundred years until the end of the seventh century were a period of great change for Japan. This does not mean that Japan took in all of China's culture, but it did learn many things from China. Using what was learned from China as a basis, Japan, in the middle of the seventh century, reformed its government. Until then, the powerful clans had their own territories and held independent power. Furthermore, they controlled their people in an authoritarian manner. However, with the reforms, the land and populace held by the powerful clans became the property of the government. It was the emperor who held political power and appointed [members of] the powerful clans to be officials of the government. Central government officials with high rank, that is, the nobility, received large amounts of land and stipends. The peasants were allotted land, and they had to pay taxes with the crops that they harvested from it. Furthermore, since they were obligated to provide labor for public works construction, the lives of the peasants were by no means easy.

Lesson 4. The Nara Period

In the beginning of the eighth century, a capital was built at Nara, modeled after the capital of China. The period when Nara was the capital is called the Nara period.

The people of the upper classes, such as the emperor and the aristocrats, led a gay and joyous life, while the lives of the masses, who were required to pay taxes, became very difficult; and anxieties began to heighten among the people. The emperor tried to calm the anxieties of the people with the strength of Buddhism. He had a temple called Todaiji erected, and there a statue of Buddha, sixteen meters or forty-five feet in height, was built. This is the famous Great Buddha of Nara. However, because it took nine years to build, the lives of the people became more and more difficult and the world was in chaos. Accordingly, the emperor abandoned the Nara capital, which had continued for about seventy years, and in the year 794 built a new capital called Heian Kyoo in present-day Kyoto.

Extensive repairs on the Great Buddha, built in the middle of the eighth century, were completed in seven years in 1980, at the great cost of $23,000,000. Horyuji, mentioned in the previous chapter, and many other temples and Buddhist images transmit the Buddhist culture that flourished long ago. These are precious cultural artifacts and are carefully preserved even today. Much later, in the Meiji period, the quiet autumnal evening of Nara was captured in a haiku by Masaoka Shiki. It is one of the haiku with which everyone is familiar:

As I eat a persimmon,
Bells of Horyuji toll.

As for the literary works of the Nara period, there are the *Kojiki,* the *Nihonshoki,* the *Manyoshu,* and others. The *Kojiki* and *Nihonshoki* are chronicles centered on the emperor, written down based on legends transmitted orally from ancient times. The *Manyoshu* is the oldest collection of poems and includes poems not only about the emperor and the aristocracy, but also about women and farmers. In the *Manyoshu,* there are many poems that are appreciated even today.

Lesson 5. The Heian Period (A): The Life of the Aristocrats

The period of about four centuries until 1185, after the capital was moved from Nara in 794 to the present Kyoto, is called the Heian period. And until 1869, when Edo, the present Tokyo, became the capital, Kyoto was the capital of Japan for nearly 1,100 years.

One of the distinctive features of the Heian period is that the aristocracy was the center of society. Because the aristocracy possessed much land, their income was large and they lived an extravagant life. It was the aristocrats who actually held political power, and not the emperor. Among the aristocrats, it was the Fujiwara clan that was especially powerful. The Fujiwara clan made their daughters empresses and their daughters' children emperors. This is how the Fujiwara clan became relatives of the emperor. Thus, from about the middle of the ninth century to the beginning of the eleventh century, the important positions in the imperial court were almost all monopolized by members of the Fujiwara clan. The Fujiwara clan built the most extravagant palace; invited the aristocrats to poetry gatherings, boating parties, and flower viewings; and every day lived a carefree life. Fujiwara Michinaga took the full moon to represent this completely satisfied life, with nothing to be desired, and wrote the following verse:

As I think this world is mine,
I lack nothing like the full moon.

There is a temple called Byodoin in Uji, Kyoto, and it was reportedly built as a villa by the Fujiwara clan. They say that the Byodoin in Kaneohe, in Hawaii, was modeled after the Byodoin in Uji, which was built in the Heian period.

Lesson 6. The Heian Period (B): From Chinese Civilization to Japanese Civilization

Another distinctive feature of the Heian period is the transfer of the Chinese culture to Japanese culture.

The aristocrats of the Nara period desired the clothing and everything else from Chinese culture, but around the middle of the ninth century, the culture imported from the T'ang, that is, China, was gradually Japanized, and a new, distinctive Japanese culture began to sprout. For example, the twelve-layered lady's ceremonial robe that we see in illustrations today is the dress of the aristocrats of the Heian period, but compared to the clothing that was imported from China, we see a big difference. Actually, it is said that the kimono that is the native costume worn by the Japanese was the clothing worn as an undergarment by the aristocrats during the Heian period.

Japan stopped sending students and envoys to China about the end of the ninth century. It was thought that there was nothing more to be learned from China.

It was during the Heian period also that the kana characters were derived from kanji. A portion of the kanji was taken to form the katakana. For example, the katakana イ was formed from the left part of the kanji 伊. In the case of hiragana, it was not a portion of a kanji but rather a simplification of the whole kanji. For example, the hiragana い was simplified from the 以 of 以上. あ was a character simplified from the 安 of 平安. The katakana ウ and the hiragana う came from the 宇 of 宇治. The katakana ウ was made from the top part of 宇, and the entire kanji was simplified to make the hiragana う.

It became easy to express Japanese because of the development of the kana characters. Thus, not only Chinese literature, but also Japanese literature began to flourish. However, at this time it was only females who wrote in hiragana; males used kanji. *Waka, nikki,* essays, and tales written in hiragana became widespread. Of these, *The Tale of Genji,* written by Murasaki Shikibu, an aristocratic lady of the early eleventh century, is famous. It is a long novel that portrays the brilliant life and sensibilities of the Heian-period aristocracy, and it is one of the most outstanding works in world literature. The original text is written in the classical language, but it has also been rendered into modern languages. And it has been translated into English as well, and is widely read.

Lesson 7. The Kamakura and Ashikaga Periods

In Kyoto, regardless of how much ability one possessed, there was no chance to succeed in life unless one was a member of the Fujiwara clan. Thus, people other than the Fujiwara clan gradually moved to the countryside. There they established their power and became powerful families.

In Kyoto, due to the neglect of political affairs by government officials, the world was in chaos. Because of that, the powerful families in the provinces had to arm themselves and protect their land and properties. This is the beginning of the samurai.

Among the samurai leaders, the most powerful ones were the Genji and the Heishi. Between the Genji and the Heishi began a power dispute. At first the Heishi won, but before long the Genji became strong, until finally, in 1185, at Dannoura near Shimonoseki, the Genji destroyed the Heishi. After seven years, in

1192, Minamoto-no-Yoritomo became the shogun and founded the shogunate in Kamakura. This is the beginning of the shogunate government of the samurai.

As for the cultural aspect, a new Buddhism for the people was born. Until the Heian period, Buddhism was for the aristocracy, but in the Kamakura period, new sects were born, and it was the Zen sect that spread among the warriors, while among the farmers it was the Jodo sect, the Jodo-shin sect, and the Nichiren sect. These are called Kamakura Buddhism.

Since the Kamakura period was a period when the warrior class flourished and the new Buddhism was born, the characteristics of this period were reflected in their literature and art. In literature, war chronicles such as the *Tale of the Heike* were written, while in art, many picture scrolls depicting warriors and priests were painted.

After the Kamakura Shogunate was overthrown in 1333, Ashikaga Takauji founded a new shogunate in Kyoto. Because the Ashikaga Shogunate was not very strong, there was no end to rebellions by the peasants and territorial disputes among the daimyo all over the country.

The Ashikaga period is also referred to as the Muromachi period. This is because it was [located] in the Muromachi [area] of Kyoto. From the standpoint of culture, the tea ceremony, flower arranging, and Noh drama flourished. Silk and cotton textiles were also produced. Nishijin in Kyoto is known for Nishijin brocade even today, and it became the center of textiles during the Muromachi period. It was also during this period that the Temple of the Golden Pavilion and the Temple of the Silver Pavilion were built.

Lesson 8. Guns and the Unification of the Whole Country

The roughly one-hundred-year period to the end of the Muromachi period, that is, from 1467 to 1573, is also called the Warring States period, and the feudal lords in various parts of Japan fought each other for territory. Just about that time, in 1543, a Portuguese ship drifted to Tanegashima Island in Kyushu. The Portuguese people on that ship had guns with them. Since the Japanese weapons at this time were the sword and the bow and arrow, [warriors] fought one against one. Thus, the feudal lords were very surprised with the new weapons that the Portuguese brought with them. With the introduction of these guns, war in Japan changed from one against one to group against group. The feudal lords who immediately adopted guns rapidly became strong. They were Oda Nobunaga, Toyotomi Hideyoshi, and Tokugawa Ieyasu.

Nobunaga, a samurai general, was very strong and was about to unify the entire country, but just before the unification, he was assassinated. After that, Toyotomi Hideyoshi, a vassal of Nobunaga's, unified the whole country in 1590, and built Osaka Castle. A feudal lord in the Warring States period built a castle in his territory and forced his samurai followers to live around the castle. The merchants and manufacturers were also gathered there. In this way castle towns were built in various areas of Japan. Among these castle towns, many developed as commercial centers and became the very large cities of today. Osaka is one of them.

Hideyoshi had a strong ambition and attempted to conquer China as well, but he failed.

After the arrival of the Portuguese ship on Tanegashima Island in 1543, trade with the West began. The ships arrived in Japan from the south, so at that time, the Portuguese, Spanish, and Italians were called Southern Barbarians. The Southern Barbarians brought many novel things to Japan. Along with [material] things, they also brought words. For example, words still used today, such as *tabako* (tobacco), *kasutera* (sponge cake), *pan* (bread), and so forth are loan words introduced at that time. In 1549, Christianity was also introduced. And within a period of a little more than two years, it is said that nearly one thousand people became Christians.

Lesson 9. The Edo Period (A): Isolationism and the Social System

After Hideyoshi died, Tokugawa Ieyasu won the Battle of Sekigahara and, followed by approximately three hundred daimyo, governed the whole country. In 1603 Ieyasu became the commander-in-chief and established a shogunate in Edo. The following 265-year period is called the Edo or Tokugawa period.

The Tokugawa Shogunate was fearful of the increase of believers in the Christian faith. They thought that Christians would pledge their loyalty to the Pope in Rome and not listen to the words of the feudal lords. So, in the early seventeenth century, the shogunate banned Christianity and sent all the missionaries out of the country. Only nonmissionary Dutch and Chinese were allowed to trade in Nagasaki, and all trade with other countries was prohibited. This is called *sakoku* [closed country].

The Tokugawa Shogunate clearly delineated the social classes. This is called *shi-noo-koo-shoo* [warriors, farmers, artisans, and tradesmen]. The highest class was the samurai, and they carried swords. Warriors had the privilege to cut down and kill on the spot a person who did something that was rude. The farmers and the townsmen were below the samurai. Among the townsmen were the artisans and the tradesmen. The artisans were the people who made things. The tradesmen were those who were engaged in buying and selling.

The respective classes [to which people were assigned] were decided at the time of birth, and one could not change his job or the place where he lived at will. One could not even marry someone out of his class. If one happened to be born into a farming household, he had to farm even if he disliked it. If one's parents were samurai, a boy could boast and carry swords, even if he were a fool. Samurai, farmers, and townsmen were all segregated according to their respective dress and even separate speech styles.

According to the records, the population of the Tokugawa period was 84 percent farmers, 7 percent samurai, and 6 percent townsmen. A farmer received rice fields from his daimyo to cultivate rice, and altogether had to pay one half of his harvest as taxes to the daimyo. Since the taxes were so heavy, the average farmer did not have an easy life. Even if he grew rice, he himself could seldom eat it. The samurai lived by eating the rice collected from the farmers and also by exchanging the rice for cash in the market place.

Lesson 10. The Edo Period (B): Learning, Industry, and the Culture of the Townspeople

Confucianism from China was propagated among the daimyo and the samurai by the shogunate. Confucianism emphasized morality, and because it taught a retainer to give his loyalty to his master and that children must be devoted to their parents, it was a convenient teaching for the shogunate.

In the middle of the eighteenth century, however, there appeared people who criticized such policies of the shogunate as isolationism and the class system of warrior, farmer, artisan, and tradesman. And the classical studies of Japanese history and language before the influence of Buddhism and Confucianism were completed. Further, Western studies of astronomy, medicine, and other European science gradually became popular. Even among the children of farmers and merchants, [the numbers of] those going to temple schools to learn to read, write, and use the abacus suddenly increased. At this time, Japan became the country with the most thriving education [activity] in the world.

In industry, by the eighteenth century, silk and cotton textiles, pottery, and lacquerware in many areas of the country came to be thriving businesses. For example, the famous Nishijin weaving of Kyoto, the porcelain of Owari, and the Wajima lacquerware of Noto started to flourish from this period. As industries grew, Osaka and Edo developed as commercial cities.

As business prospered and the lives of the merchants became prosperous, the culture of the townspeople began to flourish. From the latter half of the seventeenth century until the eighteenth century, culture flourished in all its variety: haiku, *ukiyoe,* puppet dramas, Kabuki, and the like. Matsuo Basho wrote many superb haiku. Ihara Saikaku wrote novels and described the life of the townspeople living within a strict status system and rules. Chikamatsu Monzaemon wrote puppet dramas and Kabuki plays. The theaters prospered in Edo and Osaka. Today, the Kabuki and puppet dramas that have been preserved as representative Japanese art forms flourished during the Edo period as amusements for the commoners.

The *ukiyoe* portrayed the manners and customs of the Edo period. As for the artists of *ukiyoe,* Hiroshige (famous for the "Fifty-three Stages of the Tokaido"), Utamaro (for his drawings of beautiful women), Sharaku (for his many drawings of actors with their distinctive facial expressions and hands), and others are widely known.

Lesson 11. The Meiji Period Following the Meiji Restoration

As discontent with the Tokugawa Shogunate grew, there emerged many people who thought it would be better to overthrow the shogunate and, as in former times, entrust the government to the emperor. Further, in the mid-nineteenth century, the countries of the West were beginning to show interest in trading with Japan. Then, from the middle of the nineteenth century, starting with the U.S., trade with countries like Russia, England, and France began. Gradually, society changed, and the movement to overthrow the shogunate grew. The Tokugawa shogun finally submitted, and in 1867 returned authority to the emperor. Thus ended the long Tokugawa period. Government by the samurai was over and the Meiji period began. Japan was newly reborn.

Meiji means "enlightened government." Edo was renamed Tokyo, and the emperor moved from Kyoto to Tokyo. Tokyo became the capital of Japan. The class system of warrior, farmer, artisan, and merchant was abolished. The samurai disappeared as well, and everyone became equal. People were able to choose of their own will their occupation and place of residence. They were also free to marry anyone. And, people could become Christians freely.

Industries like coal mining and spinning also developed. Railroads, electric lights, telephones, postal service, newspapers, and magazines became available. Nationwide, elementary schools were founded. Middle schools, high schools, and colleges were also established, and even the children of farmers could go to college.

There were also many great men. Fukuzawa Yukichi wrote, in his book *Gakumon no susume* (The Encouragement of Learning), "Heaven made no man superior to another, nor inferior to another," and he taught people freedom and equality.

In literature, Shimazaki Toson, Mori Ogai, Natsume Soseki, Ishikawa Takuboku, and others appeared and wrote works describing the lives of the people and the society of the time. These are widely read even today.

In the fine arts, Western painting was introduced, and great artists appeared.

In music, Western songs like "The Glow of the Firefly" [Auld Lang Syne] were introduced, and orchestral concerts were also held. Among the composers, Taki Rentaro has bequeathed to us "The Moon Over the Old Castle" and numerous other great pieces.

Because the new culture continued to sprout in this way, it was called "Civilization and Enlightenment." People's lives were modernized. The people of that time expressed the change in society, saying, "If you tap the cropped head, you can almost hear the sound of civilization and enlightenment." Cutting off the *"chonmage"* [topknot] and replacing it with short hair, wearing Western clothes, and putting on shoes, the Japanese, who had not eaten beef, were now drinking milk and eating *sukiyaki.*

In the period of only half a century, after the opening of the country in 1854 until the death of Emperor Meiji, Japan changed from a feudalistic, agricultural country to an important, modern, industrial country of the world. Such remarkable progress is unparalleled in world history.

Lesson 12. Modern Times

From the Meiji period on, that is, the Meiji, Taisho, Showa, and the present Heisei period, is called "Modern Times," and Japan fought and won wars first with China and then with Russia [during this period]. In 1910, Korea was made a colony of Japan. Gradually, Japan's territory was enlarged, and about 1919, Japan became one of the great powers of the world.

Through military strength, Japan's domain was expanded, and as it came to be recognized as a powerful nation, the military faction gradually became arrogant and began to run the government. Consequently, Japan slowly became a militaristic country, and in 1931, Japan invaded China. The U.S. disapproved of Japan's invasion of China and refused to trade with Japan.

On December 8, 1941 (the morning of December 7 in Honolulu), Japan attacked Pearl Harbor and started a war with the U.S. Because of this war, Okinawa was changed into a battleground; atomic bombs were dropped on Nagasaki and Hiroshima; and Tokyo became a field of destruction. In 1945, on the 15th of August, Japan finally surrendered. Thus, World War II came to an end.

The fact that many sacrificed their lives in the war is sad, but since the war, Japan has been reborn to become a democratic nation. Armaments were discarded, and under a new Constitution, Japan proceeded as a peaceful nation with equality for men and women, with guaranteed freedom and individual rights. Manufacturing industries as well developed rapidly, and Japan today has come to be called an economic giant.

In literature, many writers have produced many excellent works. Kawabata Yasunari, who wrote *Snow Country,* received the Nobel Prize for Literature in 1968. Translated literature also flourishes, and almost all of the outstanding literature from foreign countries has been translated into Japanese and is widely read.

Lesson 13. The Constitution of Japan and Democratic Government

After the war, the constitution that had been written during the Meiji period was revised, and the Constitution of Japan was begun anew. Before the war, the Emperor had great powers, and the rights and freedom of the people were quite restricted. After the Constitution was revised, the Emperor, who had been the sovereign of the country, was changed to the symbol of the state. And in the new Constitution, in accordance with the democratic way of thinking, the following three points are clarified as special features.

First, the supreme power to decide on government policies is with the people. Namely, through elections, the people choose their representatives, and the elected representatives, as members of the Diet, decide on government policies by majority rule.

Second, the Constitution establishes the rights of freedom and equality for all of the people. The freedom of thought and religion, the freedom to express one's ideas in publications and the like, the freedom to choose one's own residence and occupation, the freedom to hold meetings and form associations, and so on are guaranteed by the Constitution.

Third, it resolves never to engage in war.

After the war, in accordance with the new Constitution, Japan put democratic government into practice. The country's government is operated by three governmental organs: the Diet, the Cabinet, and the Court of Justice. The nation's power is divided among three bodies, and these three, respectively, perform a share of the work so that no one authority will become stronger [than the others].

The Diet is the country's supreme political organ, and the making of laws is its chief work. The structure of the Diet is that it is made up of two houses, the House of Representatives and the House of Councillors. The members are all selected by election. The tenure of office for the House of Representatives is four years and for the House of Councillors is six years. The political parties that have seats in the Diet today are ten, but the main ones are the Liberal Democratic Party, the Japan Socialist Party, the Clean Government Party, the Democratic Socialist Party, and the Japan Communist Party. The one with the largest number of members is the Liberal Democratic Party, which has held political power straight through since 1948.

The Cabinet is composed of the ministers (such as the Ministers of State and the Cabinet Prime Minister) of each ministry—the Ministry of Foreign Affairs, the Ministry of Finance, the Ministry of Education, and the rest. The Prime Minister is selected from within the party with the most members and is named by the Diet. The other ministers are appointed by the Prime Minister. The Cabinet is the organ that actually carries out policy, according to the laws and the budget decided by the Diet. This is commonly called the administration.

The duty of the Court of Justice is to decide whether the laws, instructions, regulations, and so forth comply with the Constitution. Further, in accordance with the law, it is the work of the Court of Justice to judge criminal offenses and to solve various problems of society and the home.

Lesson 14. Industrial Development and Foreign Trade

With 84 percent of the population as farmers during the Edo period, Japan, for a long time going back to antiquity, has had agriculture as an important industry; however, today households in agriculture are only about 10 percent. Japan's major industry has changed from agriculture to manufacturing.

Japan's industry had been progressing since before the war, and for some time after the war, emphasis was still on light industries like the textile industry. In 1947, 75 percent of the export commodities were textile products. Today, export commodities are almost all heavy industrial products.

In Japan in the 1960s, the machinery and chemical industries developed rapidly. Japan had adopted America's advanced technology and learned the "know-how." It then made the latest equipment, and rapidly produced good-quality products. During the first half of the 1970s, due to the oil crisis, there were a few years of recession, but before long, conditions once again improved, and in recent years, robots have been introduced, and the machinery production for the auto and other industries has shown even higher levels of growth. Japan has come to be called an economic giant.

Influenced by the oil crisis, even in America the [numbers of] people who prefer small cars have increased, and the Japanese car, which has met the needs of the times, has become the top export commodity. Japanese cars have a good reputation because they get along with less gas and cause little trouble.

A really good product cannot be expected with good equipment alone, however. Japanese workers make every effort to manufacture the best product for their company, and they take pride in their company. The company managers take great care of the workers who work hard for the company. In Japan one is never fired unless one has done something really bad. During good or bad times, the management and the workers become one and do their best. Products of good quality are made in this way.

There has been deep interest in this kind of system of Japanese enterprise, and in recent years specialists from America, an advanced country, have come to Japan to study [Japanese] know-how.

Modern Japan has thus developed its industry and is exporting all kinds of products to developed and developing countries: superior-quality machines, such as automobiles, ships, bicycles, motorcycles, tape recorders, televisions, radios, watches, computers, and so on, as well as iron and steel, chemical products, and textile products. Moreover, in addition to these products, the export of [industrial] plants and the technology related to them is also increasing.

However, because Japan is lacking in natural resources, raw materials have to be imported from America, Saudi Arabia, Indonesia, and other countries to manufacture these products. The distinctive feature of Japan's foreign trade is that the import share of crude petroleum and various raw materials is very high, but the import share of manufactured goods is low.

Lesson 15. School Life

Monday through Saturday, Japanese children go to school. In Japan it is generally not customary for parents (by car) or a school bus to transport the children. If the school is far, trains or buses are used, but in the case of public schools, even if they are far, the schools in the districts that children go to are only a distance of about a thirty-minute walk. The neighborhood children call on each other and walk together to school.

At the schools, the children have everyday responsibilities besides their studies. After the day's lessons are over, the students clean the classrooms inside and out, the schoolyard, the restrooms, and so on. To keep one's surroundings beautiful is the responsibility of those on cleanup duty.

In the intermediate and high schools especially, after-school club activities are vigorous. Besides sports clubs like [those for] baseball, tennis, table tennis, volleyball, kendo, karate, swimming, and so on, there are various other clubs for English, drama, calligraphy, forensics, flower arrangement, tea ceremony, chorus, piano, brass band, and so on. The students join the clubs that they like and participate in the activities.

Some of the enjoyable things about school life are the spring and autumn excursions, the sports day, and the school excursions scheduled in the last year of the elementary, intermediate, and high schools.

For most intermediate and high-school students, the biggest worry is the entrance examination to a high school or university. Most intermediate-school graduates enter high school, and about half of the high-school graduates enter either junior college or a university; the majority of those who aspire to enter a school [of a higher level] commute, after school is out, to private ["cram"] schools, for which they pay a high monthly tuition, or study under a private tutor for the entrance examinations.

After high-school graduation, there are those who do not go to a junior college or a university, but go to sewing school, nursing school, or other professional schools to learn a technical skill.

In addition, in Japan, besides the regular high schools, there are commercial high schools, technical high schools, fisheries high schools, and agriculture and forestry high schools, and so forth. Such high schools are geared mainly for those who hope to work right after graduation.

With homework and entrance examination studies, there is much that is painful while one is in school, but after graduation it is the enjoyable things that continue forever afterwards: intermediate schools, high schools, and universities have their respective school and class reunions and post-graduation get-togethers at least once a year. There are reminiscences of school days and exchanging of the latest news. The more time passes after graduation the more nostalgic one gets, and the parties become even more enjoyable. After twenty or thirty years, it is truly delightful to return to the old school days and reminisce together.

Lesson 16. The Modernization of Lifestyle and the New Life for Women

As of 1987, Japan's population exceeds 120,000,000, and nearly half of this number is concentrated in the principal cities of Tokyo, Osaka, and Nagoya. The total land area of these three cities is only 14 percent of the land area of all Japan; therefore, almost half of the population of Japan lives in this 14 percent of the land. When you compare the population per one square kilometer of land area [in Japan] with the U.S., in the U.S. it is calculated at just twenty, while in Japan it is over three hundred persons. This in fact is the average for the population of Japan as a whole; thus, in the large cities it probably is much greater than this.

The rapid growth of industry in the 1960s was accompanied by a sudden increase in the population of the cities. The [number of] people in agriculture declined, and the former paddy and farm lands turned rapidly into residential areas; here and there, housing developments were born, the communities on the outskirts of the large cities became bedroom towns, and the number of white-collar workers and "office ladies" who spend one to two hours to commute by train or car to work increased.

Industralization changed the lives of the people greatly. The washing machine, refrigerator, color television, vacuum cleaner, air conditioner, automobile, electronic range, and many other electrical appliances came into the home, and the lifestyle was rapidly modernized. Accordingly, the work that was previously done largely by hand is now done by machine. Computations previously done by abacus are now done by a calculator. People were especially amazed at the word processor, which appeared during the latter half of the 1970s. In Japan up to that time, because there was no convenient machine that anyone could use like the English typewriter, the Japanese had to write letters and everything else by hand; however, with the introduction of the word processor, documents could be written neatly. High-performance new models of word processors for office use and even portable word processors are being sold one after another. A word processor that can print not only kana or kanji but also, with a simple change of key, even English writing can be purchased for about the same price as an English typewriter.

In addition, what has improved immensely because of the modernization of lifestyle is the life of the housewife. Unlike the Japan of the period when it was an agrarian country, when every household required extra hands, the average number of people per family today has decreased to 3.3 persons. In other words, there are only one or two children per family. With the smaller number of children and with improvements in living, free time for the housewife has increased.

As a result, the number of women working part-time has increased remarkably in recent years. There is a general tendency for Japanese women to stop working after getting married and devote themselves to housework and caring for the children, but today, when the children start school and require less care, more and more women seem to have gone back to work again. Today this type of working couple is on the increase; for the housewife, it is convenient to have a job where one works part-time four to six hours per day. According to recent statistics, it seems more women feel that life is more meaningful when one does some work outside.

As lifestyle improves and free time increases—and this is not limited to women—those who enjoy leisure time have increased. As for hobbies, there are golf, travel, and various other things, but in recent years there has been a great boom in *karaoke* singing.

Lesson 17. Traditional Culture in a Modern Society

As we have seen thus far, the Japanese in ancient times learned from China, and then learned many things from Europe and the United States, especially since the advent of the modern era. The Japanese have changed what they have learned from other countries to suit themselves, and skillfully combining these things with what they already possessed, have adopted them into their own lives.

For example, in the matter of religion, there are, of course, specific religions and followers of different sects, but a great many Japanese practice the ceremonies at the time of birth according to Shinto, and hold funeral services at the time of death according to the Buddhist religion. Weddings are conducted according to either Shinto or the Christian religion. Thus, the Japanese do not possess a fixed religious consciousness or attitude, and the number who have adopted Shinto, Buddhism, or Christianity into their lives—for the ceremony, with no relation to their religious faith—is extremely large.

The lifestyle as well of present-day Japan is a blend of Japanese and Western. Lately, the construction of homes and condominiums has been described in terms of "two DK" or "three LDK." "DK" in Japan means a dining-kitchen with table and chairs, a kitchen where meals are eaten. "L" means a living room and is generally a Western-style room with a carpet and a sofa, used as a drawing room when there is a guest. The number in front indicates the number of other rooms. A two DK may have two rooms with mats and sliding doors in the Japanese style, and a three LDK may have only one Japanese room. The DK is Western-style, and the children's room usually has desks, chairs, and a double bunk-bed, so it can be said that nearly all Japanese homes today are a blend of Japanese and Western styles. In the cities, the washroom is generally a Western-style toilet, and of course it flushes. However, to prevent the wasting of water, an apparatus in the water tank is designed so that the water for washing the hands is then used to flush the toilet. The bath is Japanese-style. The hot water in the tub is not changed each time, and the whole family uses the same water. Therefore, one never uses soap or washes oneself in the tub. The Japanese, who love to soak up the heat at leisure, will not exchange the traditional deep bathtub for the shallow Western one. Furthermore, the bath and the toilet are always separated.

Even eating habits are a blend of Japanese and Western. Steak is the favorite of most Japanese, and among the young people living a city life, toast and coffee are preferred to rice and miso soup for breakfast.

As for clothing, it has changed from Japanese to Western since the war. The kimono, which is the Japanese native costume, cannot be separated from the tea ceremony, the Japanese dance, Kabuki, and other traditional culture. Besides, the Japanese are a people who place great weight on ceremony and formality, and the kimono gives life to this formality; so there are various conventions that must be observed according to the seasons, occasions, human relationships, and age. Thus, the kimono, which reflects the spiritual culture of the Japanese, can be said to be the most appropriate costume at times when there are formal occasions such as the various ceremonies, receptions, and so on. However, for everyday wear, convenience is primary, so compared to Japanese clothing, Western dress, which is simple to manipulate and easy to move around in, has definitely become a fixture of the daily lives of the Japanese. Moreover, particularly for young women, a kimono is a very special thing to wear. A complete formal kimono, which costs from three to five thousand dollars, is worn with pride and joy once or twice a year, at such times as whenever one is invited to a wedding reception, or New Year's Day, or a coming-of-age ceremony, or a college graduation exercise.

Thus, the harmony between the old and the new—this is Japanese culture.

RESOURCE MATERIALS ON JAPAN

There are many motion picture films and video cassettes from the Ministry of Foreign Affairs and the Japan National Tourist Organization on the culture and society of Japan. Some of these may possibly be available at a local Japanese Consulate. The following is a list of some of the current video cassettes as of fall 1988.

Culture and Sports of Japan

The Doll Master and His Apprentice	30 min.
The Carp Town	30 min.
Japan Today	30 min.
Japanese Cooking: A Taste for All Seasons	30 min.
Japanese Children Throughout the Year	25 min.
Sumo	15 min.
Judo	15 min.
Kendo	15 min.
Karatedo	15 min.
Aikido	15 min.
The Theater Lives	30 min.
Daichi no Mai: Traditional Japanese Dance	40 min.
Dear Uncle Kyara . . .	30 min.
The Kimono	24 min.
Ennosuke III: Kabuki Actor	35 min.
Flight from the Marshes	37 min.
Ikebana	20 min.
Kyoto: Scenes and Festivals	25 min.

Children's Stories — 90 min.

1. The Crane and the Boy
2. Kaguyahime
3. The Grateful Crane
4. Warashibe Choja

Education — 90 min.

1. Primary and Secondary Education
2. An Elementary School Teacher
3. School Days in Japan

Classical Theaters of Japan — 90 min.

1. Kabuki: The Classical Theater of Japan
2. Noh Drama
3. Bunraku: Puppet Theater of Japan

Children — 60 min.

1. Inventive Young Minds
2. Children of the Snow Country
3. Children in Towns and Villages

Music — 60 min.

1. Music of Modern Japan
2. Kitaro (Synthesizer Musician)

Architecture	60 min.
1. Japanese Architecture 2. Kisho Kurokawa	
Japanese Gardens	45 min.
1. Landscape Gardener 2. Gardens of Japan	
Ikebana II	45 min.
1. Ikebana: Art of Flower Arrangement 2. The Art and Meaning of Ikebana	
Martial Arts	30 min.
1. Budo: The Martial Arts 2. The Art of Karate	
Miscellaneous	52 min.
1. Yuzen Kimono 2. Japanese Gardens 3. Bamboo 4. Japanese Hand-Made Paper	
Manyo no Kaisan Part I (VHS only; Japanese narration)	60 min.
Manyo no Kaisan Part II (VHS only; Japanese narration)	60 min.
Manyo no Kaisan Part III (VHS only; Japanese narration)	60 min.
Manyo no Kaisan Part IV (VHS only; Japanese narration)	60 min.
Manyo no Kaisan Part V (VHS only; Japanese narration)	60 min.
Manyo no Kaisan Part VI (VHS only; Japanese narration)	60 min.
Travel	
Holiday in Japan	30 min.
Japan: Journey of Discovery	20 min.
Japan: Land of Enchantment	30 min.
Four Seasons	90 min.
A Cultural Journey into Japan; Japan: A Portrait in Sound	54 min.
The Four Seasons in Japan; This Year We Went to Japan	51 min.
Industry and Economics	
Open to the World	30 min.
Farming Techniques	90 min.
Industry, Quality Control, and Small Businesses	90 min.
Fishery and Marine Industries	60 min.
Education and Business Schools	60 min.
Agricultural Cooperatives and Farming Life	30 min.

The Japanese People and Their Activities

Profile of a Nation (miniseries)

Series 1 90 min.

1. The Useful Telephone
2. Shinkansen: Japanese Superexpress Train
3. We Sell Everything: The Japanese Department Store
4. Inventive Young Minds
5. Where the Policeman Lives
6. The Fire Fighters

Series 2 105 min.

1. Children of the Snow Country
2. A District Nurse
3. Learning a Trade
4. Children in Nursery School
5. Keeping the City Clean
6. Harvesting the Sea
7. The Local Post Office

Series 3 90 min.

1. Alternative Energy Resource
2. Recycling
3. Disaster Prevention
4. Sabo: Erosion Control
5. Vocational Training
6. The Tokyo Subway System

Series 4 105 min.

1. The Japan Overseas Cooperation Volunteers
2. The Battle Against Disease
3. Agricultural Cooperatives and Farm Life
4. Tsukuba Academic New Town
5. The Elementary School Teacher
6. Mobile Service
7. Budo: The Martial Arts

Series 5 90 min.

1. Small-Scale Urban Industries
2. JICA: Welcoming Technical Trainees from Abroad
3. The Municipal Office and Its Services
4. Fish Foods for All Tastes
5. Farming in All Seasons
6. Robots at Work

Series 6 105 min.

1. A Japanese Policewoman
2. Protecting Japan's Forests
3. Kangofu: The Japanese Nurse
4. Oyama-cho: A Village Reborn
5. A Young Worker

6. Soroban: Traditional Calculator of Japan
7. Takuhaiban: Door-to-Door Across the Nation

Series 7—Japan in General 120 min.

1. Japan: An Overview
2. Geography and Industries
3. Today's Japan
4. The Sea: Lifeline for Today and Tomorrow

Series 8—Health 90 min.

1. A District Nurse
2. The Japanese Nurse
3. The Battle Against Disease
4. Mobile Service
5. Floating Medical Clinic

Series 9—Disaster Prevention 45 min.

1. The Fire Fighters
2. Disaster Prevention
3. Sabo: Erosion Control

Series 10—Municipalities 45 min.

1. The Municipal Office and Its Services
2. Oyama-cho: A Village Reborn
3. Toga: Village for Theater

Series 11—Waste Disposal 30 min.

1. Keeping the City Clean
2. Recycling

Series 12—Economic Cooperatives 30 min.

1. JOCV: The Japan Overseas Cooperation Volunteer
2. JICA: Welcoming Technical Trainees from Abroad

Series 13—Telephone and Mail 30 min.

1. The Useful Telephone
2. The Local Post Office

Series 14—Law Enforcement 30 min.

1. Where the Policeman Lives
2. A Japanese Policewoman

Series 15 45 min.

1. Doctors to Be
2. Festival Time
3. Housing Community

Series 16 45 min.

1. "Eating Out": Restaurants Today
2. Urban Transportation
3. Sports: In the Spirit of Youth

Series 17 45 min.

1. Publishing the News
2. Students from Abroad
3. Traditions Today

Series 18 45 min.

1. Supermarkets
2. Greening the Environment
3. The Textiles of Nishijin

(NOTE: The series numbers above are provided by the authors, for the convenience of the reader; they are not the producer's own numbers.)

Business

The following video cassette tapes are from the television series *Business Nippon,* produced by the Keizai Koho Center (Japanese Institute for Social and Economic Affairs) and Japan Cable Television. Each tape runs approximately thirty minutes, and all are available in VHS and Beta formats.

No.	Title	Contents
Business Nippon—*Series I (1985)*		
038	Japan's Distribution System	Short historical background. Analysis of Japan's distribution system, including the wholesale structure, trading practices, and human relations. (November 1980)
074	Keys to Success in the Japanese Market	Japan has been accused of not being open to foreign companies. We interview three executives to find out the truth and how they have endeavored to become successful in the Japanese market. (August 1981)
077	Communication Gap	This issue focuses upon the "Communication Gap" which exists between Japan and other industrial nations, in a round table discussion. (September 1981)
086	Japanese Management	Japanese management, trade imbalances, and misunderstandings were among the key topics of discussion in the year 1981. Three businessmen from Japan, the U.S., and Europe offer their observations. (December 1981)
105	Making It in Japan: Can It Be Done?	In this program four Americans—two men and two women—talk about the problems they face in their day-to-day encounters with Japanese colleagues and clients. (August 1982)
110	Japan: Obstacles and Opportunities	The Trade Study Group is a panel of specialists who gather voluntarily to find solutions to problems between Japan and the U.S. The group has recently completed the data-based study titled "Japan: Obstacles and Opportunities," which discusses ways in which foreign businesses can enter the Japanese market. (October 1982)
116	Japanese Attitude Toward Imports	Contrary to world opinion, a survey by the Association for Promoting Imports of Manufactured Goods shows that Japan does not have a closed-door policy toward imports nor do the Japanese discriminate against foreign brands. This is further substantiated by citywide interviews with shoppers and salesclerks, who talk about the kinds of imports which appeal to them. (March 1983)

118	Japanese Industries and Robots	This program looks at the impact of industrial robots on Japan's enterprises, economy, and labor force. It examines the present situation, including some of the problems which have resulted. It also offers views on the future of robotics as it affects industry and society. (May 1983)
122	U.S. Educators Talk about Japan	Twenty U.S. educators in the Social Sciences were invited by Keizai Koho Center to get a firsthand look at Japan—its people, culture, education, and business. Most were overwhelmed by the vast information input during their limited stay. *Business Nippon* follows the group from the day of arrival to the farewell party, highlighting some of their activities including a panel discussion. (August 1983)
123	Japan's Industrial Policy	Criticisms of the Japanese Government's national industrial policy have often been heard. But they are based mainly on misunderstandings which may be used to justify trade protectionism. It is necessary to put the whole issue in a proper perspective. In this program, three panelists express their views on "Japan's Industrial Policy." (August 1983)
125	Japan's International Balance of Payments	Considerable overseas criticisms have been directed at Japan's large trade surplus as a major cause of economic friction. But up until a few years ago, Japan suffered from an excess of payments over receipts in its current accounts. Gene Gregory, professor of International Business at Sophia University in Tokyo, gives us important factors to consider regarding the international balance of payments. (October 1983)
128	Foreign Affiliated Companies: Practice Makes Perfect	Foreign affiliated companies (FACs) in Japan face numerous problems, but none which cannot be worked out or overcome with a certain amount of diplomacy, willingness, and perseverance. This program presents three small- and medium-sized businesses which have prospered in Japan. They all attest to the fact that it's not an easy road, but one which is well worth venturing on. (December 1983)
130	Taro-san at Work and Play	Taro-san, the Japanese "Everyman," is a creation of the widely syndicated political cartoonist Ranan Lurie. Just as Taro-san is not "typical," neither is the star of this program, Mr. Kumada. However, he represents a new breed of Japanese businessmen who are part of the upward mobility group: well-educated, ambitious, and dedicated. (February 1984)
134	Japanese Investments in the U.S.A.	With the number of Japanese companies that invest overseas rapidly increasing, this program examines their role in the U.S. The American production of Japanese brands is discussed through three Japanese companies. (May 1984)
135	Accessing the Japanese Market	How often have you heard the cry that it is impossible to break into the Japanese market? Though there are obviously hurdles to overcome, many of the criticisms voiced about accessing the Japanese market are based on misapprehension, and many of the failures are the result of trying too hard to do the wrong things. *Business Nippon* this week uses the recent German Fair to examine the problems and possibilities of doing business in this country. (May 1984)

140	ASEAN Trade Expansion: A Foothold in Japan	Japan has always relied on ASEAN and its neighbors to provide some of the much needed natural resources and other primary products. But with the industrialization of those countries, Japan is increasingly being counted on to buy a wide range of manufactured goods from them. In order to make ASEAN products more attractive to Japanese consumers, various suggestions are offered by marketing specialists and importers. (September 1984)
141	The Aging Society: Impact on Marketing	The number of senior citizens is rapidly increasing, and with the Japanese life span among the longest in the world, many people are becoming concerned about the quality of life after retirement. Meanwhile, businesses are custom-tailoring their products and services to attract the "silver-grey market." *Business Nippon* explores this phenomenon from the business point of view. (October 1984)
146	The Japanese Housewife: Working Part-time	More and more Japanese housewives are joining the part-time labor force. What are their reasons for doing so? And what impact does this have on the overall employment picture? *Business Nippon* takes a look at a day in the life of such a working housewife. (January 1985)
147	Conducive to Business: Factors for Achievement	After all that's been said and written about Japan's miraculous postwar rise out of the ashes to become an economic giant, this episode offers yet another view of how Japanese businesses continue to achieve their goals in a highly competitive world. Masaya Miyoshi, Keidanren's senior managing director, takes the microeconomic approach to analyzing the elements which contribute to the high performance of Japanese businesses. (February 1985)
150	Education: Competitive and Expensive	The cutthroat university entrance examination system and the rapidly rising costs of education are putting a strain on parents, students, and society. *Business Nippon* looks at education in "Japan: Competitive and Expensive." (May 1985)

Business Nippon—*Series II (1986)*

016	How to Penetrate the Japanese Market	Experts' advice on how to do business successfully in Japan. (January 1980)
020	How Does a Japanese Company Train Its Employees?	VTR report on NEC's language-training center. How Japanese companies train their employees. (March 1980)
070	Labor Management Relations	The relationship between a company and a labor union in Japan is said to be smooth compared with the U.S. or European counterparts. Foreign missions have been visiting Japan to study the Japanese situation. (July 1981)
083	Vitality of Japan's Small Business	"Japanese Management" applies to less than 20 percent of Japan's work force—government employees and large-company workers. What is the real strength behind the majority of workers—the small business employees who make up 80 percent of Japan's work force? (November 1981)
091	How a Japanese Company Achieves High Productivity: The Way Toyota Does It	Toyota's production system makes efficient use of all production-related factors to improve productivity and to reduce costs by eliminating waste.

097	Japanese Blue Collar Workers: A System, Not a Culture	Blue-collar workers have been a major force in Japan's rapid postwar economic growth. What motivates them? Professor Koike of Kyoto University explains that it is the system, not the culture. (May 1982)
111	Total Quality Control	Products made in Japan used to be considered cheap and of poor quality. However, that has drastically changed as cars, home appliances, precision instruments, and other products made in Japan have gained a wide reputation for high quality. That turnabout came in large part thanks to "Quality Control," and more recently, a system called "Total Quality Control." (November 1982)
115	Business Practice: The Japanese Way of Doing Business	In a survey of foreign business people in Japan, "Japanese business practice" was most frequently mentioned as the factor which they found most different from their expectations. Many things can be attributed to "business practice," and not knowing the Japanese way could hinder one from successfully participating in the Japanese market. A select panel discusses some of the problems and offers suggestions on how to deal with the differences. (March 1983)
127	High Productivity: How Matsushita Does It	The high quality and high productivity of Japanese manufactured goods have been the focus of world attention for some time. Last year, *Business Nippon* featured the Japanese auto industry. In this program, the Matsushita group is highlighted. A rare look is offered into the usually well-guarded process of electrical appliance production at Matsushita plants here and abroad. (November 1983)
142	Consumer Favorites in the Japanese Market	From the very expensive to the very cheap, several products have soared in popularity over the first half of the 1980s. *Business Nippon* explores the reasons behind the success of these products in the Japanese market, and how manufacturers are adapting to the changing moods of the Japanese people. (October 1984)
151	The Japanese and Their Views of Religion	Are the Japanese not religious—as they seem in the eyes of foreigners? *Business Nippon* presents two professors who talk about Japanese views of religion in the setting of Kamakura, the ancient capital. The audience will also be able to enjoy a tour of Kamakura in this program. (May 1985)
153	Savings and Spending	The Japanese are known to the world for their strong tendency to save. Recently, however, there have been marked signs that they are "tired with savings." Why so? *Business Nippon* reports on what is happening to saving and spending among the Japanese. (June 1985)
155	Hunting a House in Tokyo	*Business Nippon* hunts for a house in Tokyo to find out what kind of house may be available and on what conditions. The program also tries to give viewers a chance to see a variety of wonderful Japanese-style house interiors. (July 1985)
159	Challenge for Regional Development: Success in Ohita	Ohita's success in regional development is drawing world attention. The program shows how the mountainous prefecture successfully stopped depopulation and developed specialty products of its own, at the same time giving pride to the people who live there. (September 1985)

161	On the Market Soon	*Business Nippon* focuses on new technologies and products that are coming on the market in the near future. The program also examines which of them will turn out to be hits in the future. (October 1985)
164	Cracking the Japanese Market	Tetrapak, Polaroid, and Johnson and Johnson have one thing in common. They challenged the Japanese market and succeeded in getting a large market share. How did they manage such a feat? *Business Nippon* looks at their road to success. (December 1985)
168	Consumer Favorites '85	Many foreign firms have come into the Japanese market fully aware of the keen competition. This program reports on the best-selling products of 1985 in this competitive market. The program also reports on why a particular product got to be a best seller, how the product was developed, and what kind of sales policy was established. (February 1986)
169	Open Sesame at the TSE: Merrill Lynch Enters in	On February 1, 1986, six Merrill Lynch brokers made history when they walked onto the floor of the Tokyo Stock Exchange, marking the first time a foreign securities firm has traded there. Taking this opportunity, the program examines what's taking place at the TSE and its future prospects. (February 1986)
170	Challenge the Deming Prize: TQC in the Service Industry	In November 1985, the first report of its kind in Japan about TQC (total quality control) in the Japanese service industry was compiled by the Union of Japanese Scientists and Engineers. TQC is something that's taken for granted in the Japanese manufacturing industry but something just starting in the service industry. In this program, we will report on how TQC is being implemented by one Japanese hotel. (March 1986)

REFERENCES

Books

Beasly, W. G. *Modern Japan: Aspects of History, Literature and Society.* Japan: Charles E. Tuttle Co., 1980.

———. *The Modern History of Japan.* 2d ed. New York: Praeger, 1974.

Hadamitzky, Wolfgang, and Mark Spahn. *Kanji & Kana: A Handbook and Dictionary of the Japanese Writing System.* Rutland, Vermont; Tokyo: Charles E. Tuttle Co., 1981.

Hall, John Whitney. *Japan: From Prehistory to Modern Times.* New York: Dell Publishing Co., 1970.

Koyama, Keiichi. *KaTaKaNa: A Dictionary of Katakana Words.* Tokyo: Gakken, 1986.

Kuratani, Nao'omi, et al. *A New Dictionary of Kanji Usage.* Tokyo: Gakken, 1982.

Lebra-Sugiyama, Takie, and William P. Lebra. *Japanese Culture and Behavior: Selected Readings.* Honolulu, Hawaii: The University Press of Hawaii, 1974.

Pye, Michael. *The Study of Kanji.* Tokyo: Hokusei Press, 1971.

Sakade, Florence, et al. *A Guide to Reading & Writing Japanese.* Rutland, Vermont and Tokyo: Charles E. Tuttle Co., 1979.

The Japan Culture Institute. *A Hundred Things Japanese.* The Japan Culture Institute, 1975.

———. *A Hundred More Things Japanese.* The Japan Culture Institute, 1980.

Vogel, Ezra F. *Japan as Number 1: Lessons For America.* New York: Harper & Row, 1980.

Yamaguchi, Momoo, and Setsuko Kojima. *A Cultural Dictionary of Japan.* Tokyo: The Japan Times, Ltd.; Kenkyusha Printing Co., 1979.

Periodicals

Japan Pictorial (Quarterly; available from the Japanese Consulate).

The East. Tokyo and New York: The East Publications, Inc.

The Japan of Today (Available from the Japanese Consulate).

ANSWER KEYS TO EXERCISE SHEETS

Lesson 1

Exercise D.

1. c	5. b	9. f	13. i
2. g	6. h	10. m	14. d
3. j	7. n	11. e	15. a
4. l	8. o	12. k	

Lesson 2

Exercise B.

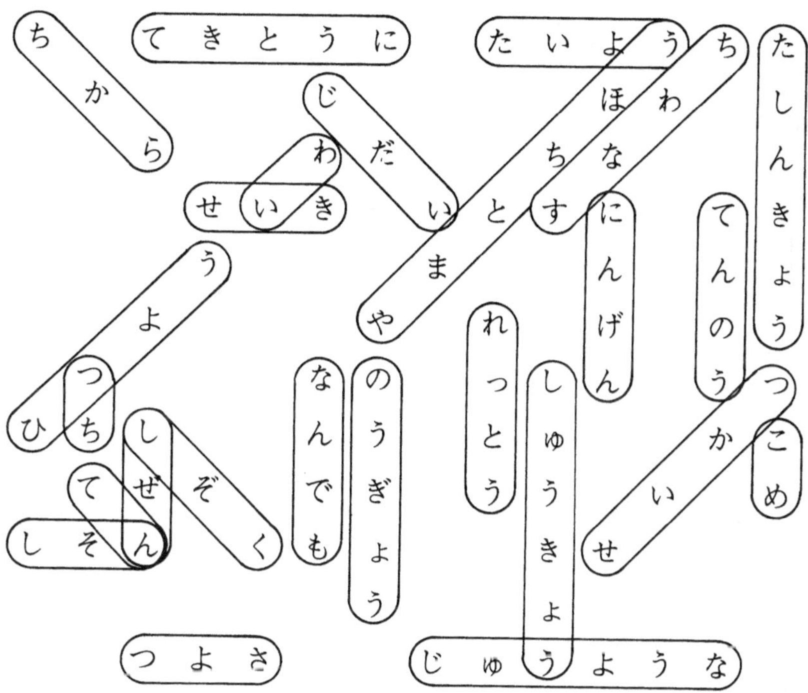

Exercise D.

1. d	5. l	9. h	13. i
2. g	6. n	10. o	14. c
3. j	7. k	11. m	15. f
4. b	8. a	12. e	

Exercise E.

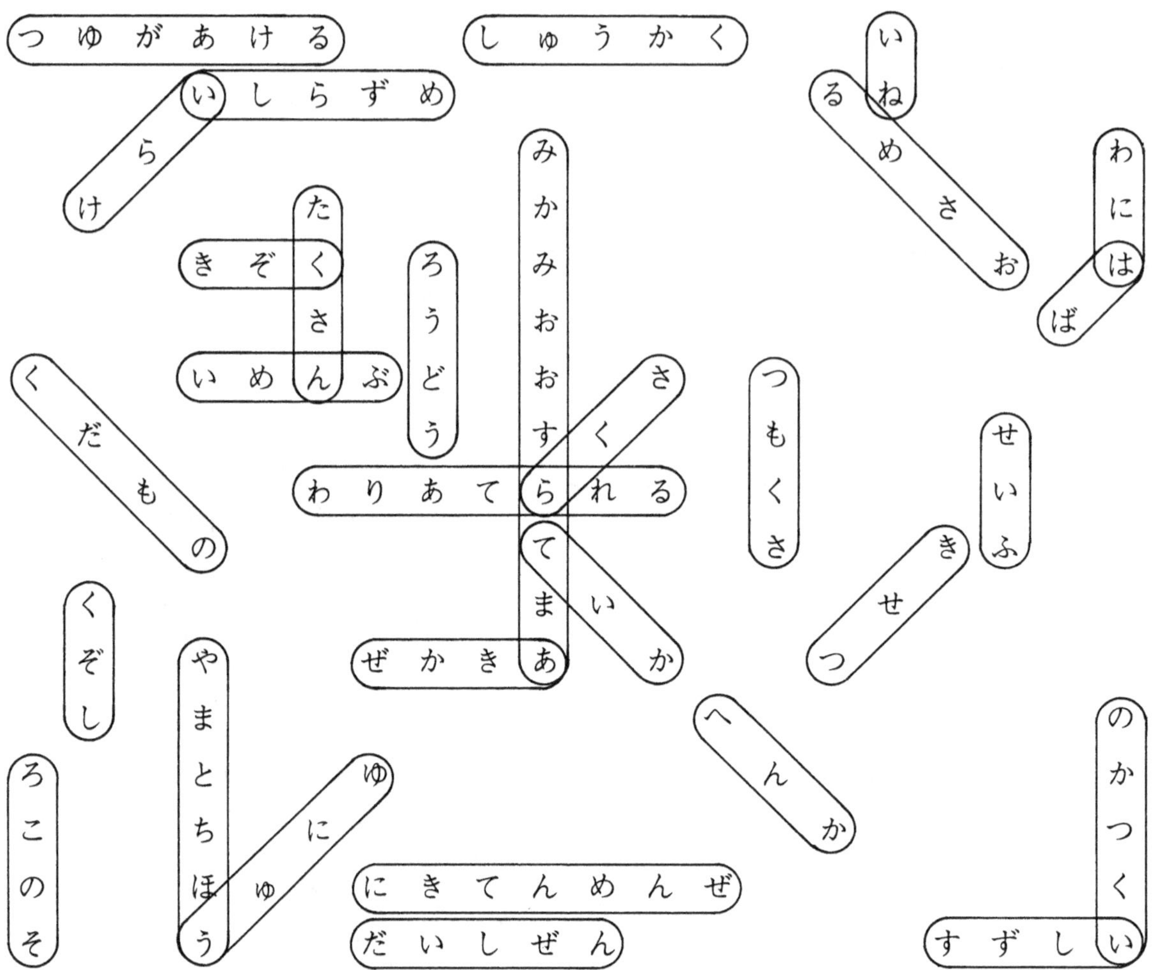

Lesson 3

Exercise B.

法	文	明	左	黒	公	事	面	全
律	道	好	交	伝	奈	良	場	面
十	二	時	代	日	通	青	前	的
常	広	期	教	労	農	民	国	月
有	正	様	本	働	業	輸	大	生
名	車	玉	功	年	通	入	歩	活
合	政	治	毎	氏	男	独	立	特
権	府	海	貴	族	心	会	間	空
力	流	川	感	在	建	築	赤	向

Exercise D.

1. d
2. f
3. b
4. j
5. l
6. h
7. o
8. m
9. i
10. g
11. p
12. a
13. n
14. c
15. k
16. e

Lesson 4

Exercise C.

だ	い	ぶ	つ		や	く		ふ			じ
	り		く					あ			ょ
	ま		り				み	ん	し	ゅ	う
	す	み	ま	せ	ん		る				り
			す			せ					ゅ
か	か	っ	た		へ	い	あ	ん	き	ょ	う
い				け		か			ぞ		し
か				れ		つ			く		ゃ
く		い	ち	ど		を		お			か
				も		す		そ		ぜ	い
た	か	さ			く	る	し	い			
	き								み	や	こ

Exercise D.

1. d
2. j
3. h
4. b
5. a
6. n
7. p
8. l
9. f
10. m
11. o
12. e
13. k
14. i
15. g
16. c

Lesson 5

Exercise C.

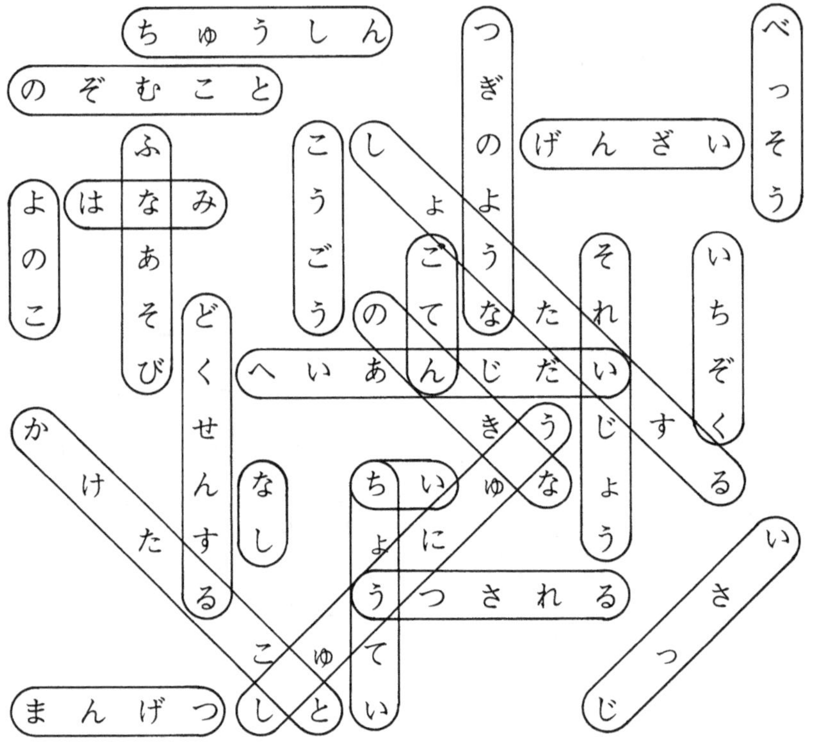

Exercise D.

1. c	5. j	9. n	13. h
2. e	6. a	10. m	14. k
3. i	7. l	11. f	15. d
4. g	8. o	12. b	16. p

Lesson 6

Exercise B.

Exercise D.

1. c	6. a	11. n	16. e
2. h	7. f	12. g	17. k
3. o	8. m	13. p	
4. l	9. q	14. b	
5. i	10. d	15. j	

Lesson 7

Exercise D.

1. e	7. u	13. x	19. v
2. i	8. k	14. h	20. f
3. m	9. w	15. j	21. d
4. g	10. p	16. t	22. r
5. b	11. c	17. l	23. q
6. n	12. a	18. o	24. s

Lesson 8

Exercise C.

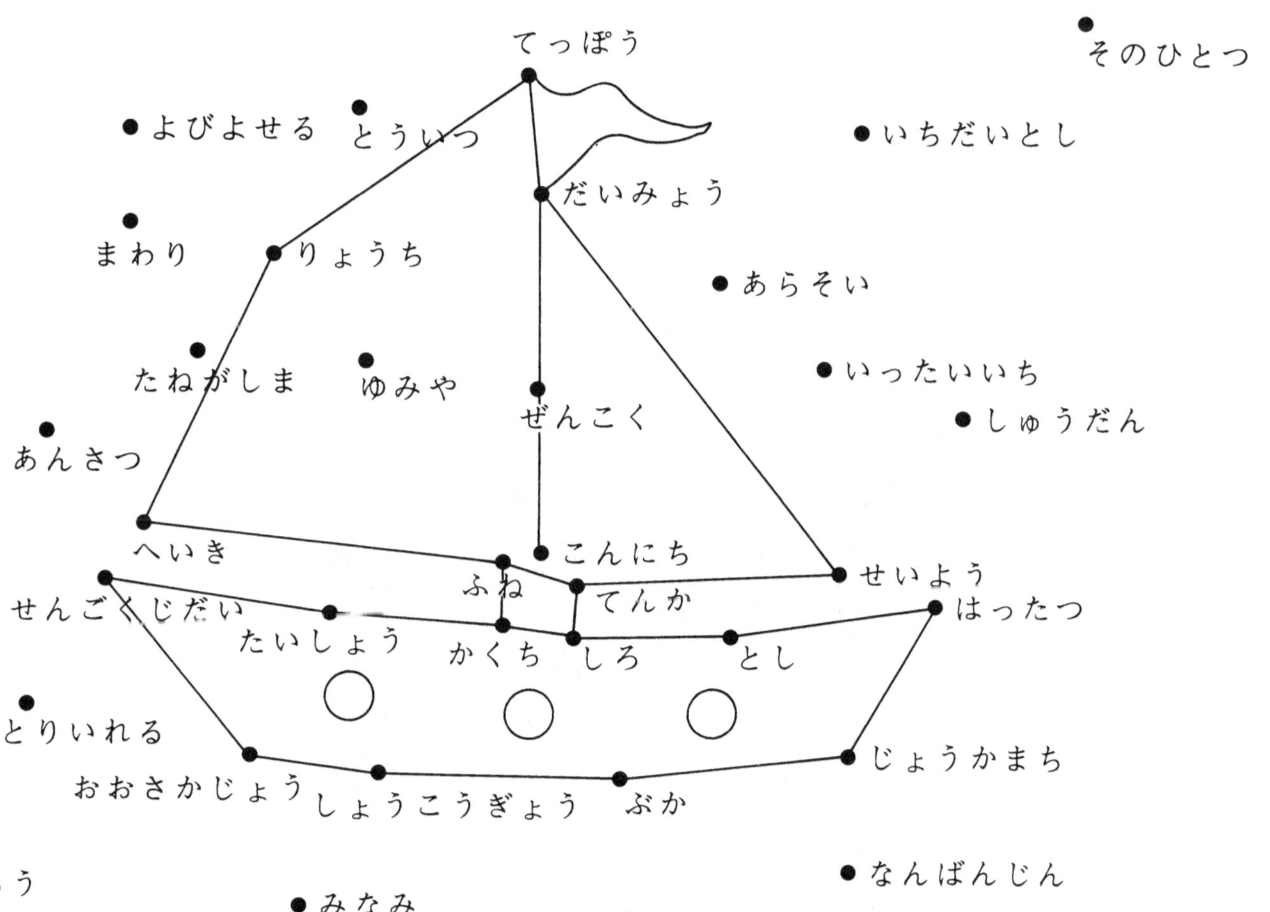

Exercise D.

1. f	6. i	11. r	16. b
2. l	7. p	12. o	17. s
3. j	8. e	13. k	18. m
4. a	9. q	14. g	19. h
5. n	10. c	15. t	20. d

Lesson 9

Exercise C.

1. d	7. m	13. h	19. v
2. w	8. k	14. q	20. j
3. i	9. u	15. c	21. o
4. g	10. s	16. l	22. e
5. p	11. a	17. t	23. n
6. b	12. r	18. f	

Exercise D.

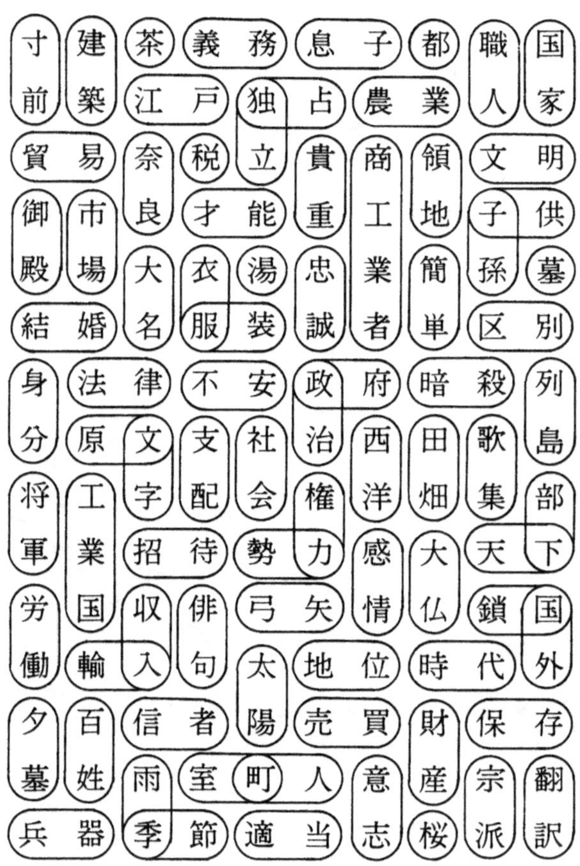

Lesson 10

Exercise D.

1. h	6. l	11. g	16. m
2. e	7. c	12. j	17. k
3. a	8. o	13. i	18. f
4. r	9. p	14. q	
5. n	10. d	15. b	

Lesson 11

Exercise C.

1. e	6. l	11. n	16. d
2. r	7. a	12. p	17. g
3. k	8. m	13. j	18. i
4. q	9. f	14. b	
5. o	10. c	15. h	

Lessons 1–11

Review Exercise

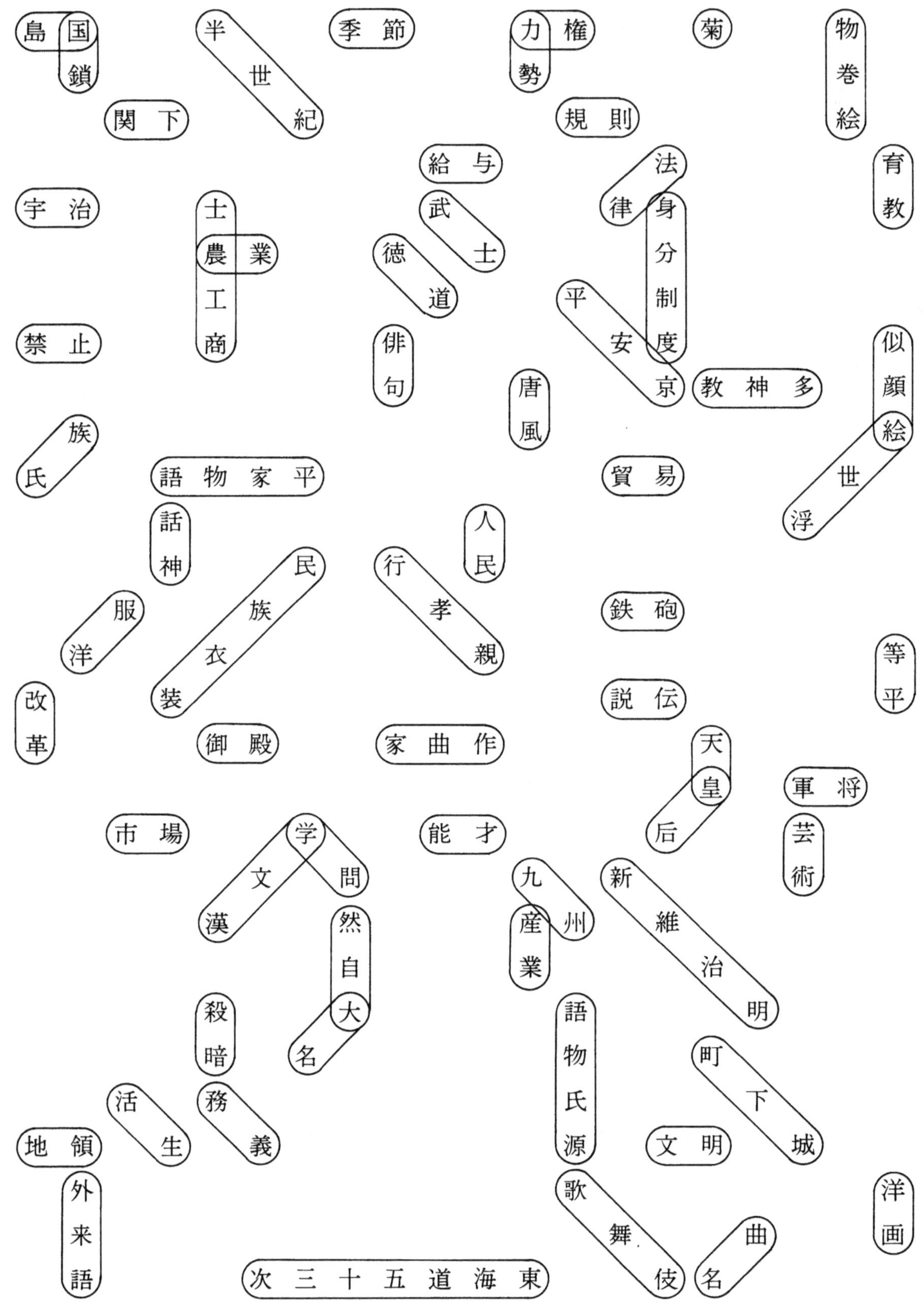

Lesson 12

Exercise C.

1. g	6. i	11. t	16. h
2. j	7. s	12. l	17. a
3. n	8. m	13. p	18. f
4. b	9. o	14. d	19. k
5. q	10. e	15. r	20. c

Lesson 13

Exercise C.

1. g	6. p	11. q	16. h
2. l	7. i	12. o	17. a
3. n	8. r	13. f	18. e
4. c	9. m	14. t	19. d
5. j	10. s	15. b	20. k

Lesson 14

Exercise B.

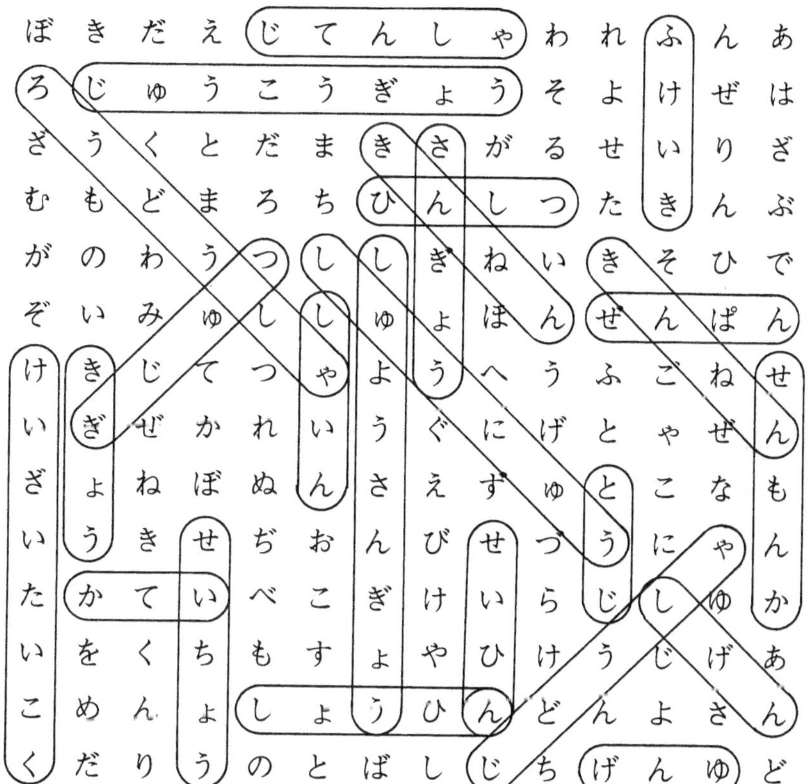

Exercise D.

1. d	6. l	11. q	16. h
2. i	7. j	12. r	17. c
3. n	8. o	13. a	18. g
4. s	9. b	14. k	19. m
5. p	10. t	15. e	20. f

Lesson 15

Exercise C.

1. c	5. i	9. g	13. d
2. h	6. b	10. l	
3. f	7. j	11. a	
4. k	8. m	12. e	

Lesson 16

Exercise B.

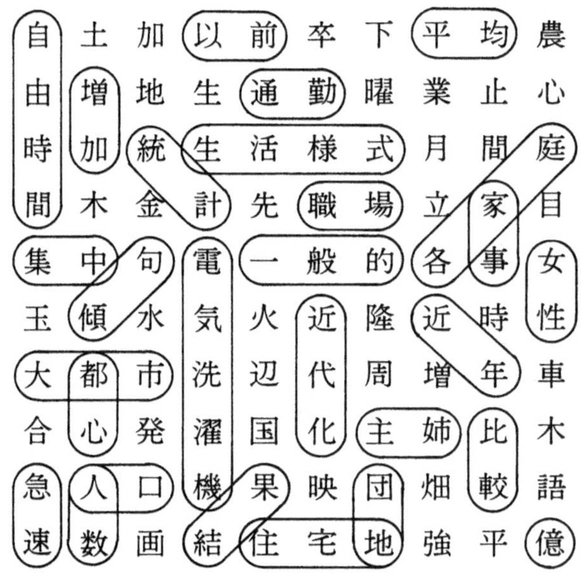

Exercise C.

1. d	6. n	11. s	16. h
2. p	7. b	12. a	17. m
3. j	8. q	13. i	18. t
4. g	9. e	14. f	19. r
5. o	10. k	15. l	20. c

Lesson 17

Exercise C.

1. f	6. l	11. n	16. g
2. q	7. i	12. a	17. j
3. d	8. t	13. e	18. p
4. m	9. b	14. k	19. h
5. o	10. s	15. c	20. r

Lessons 12–17

Review Exercise

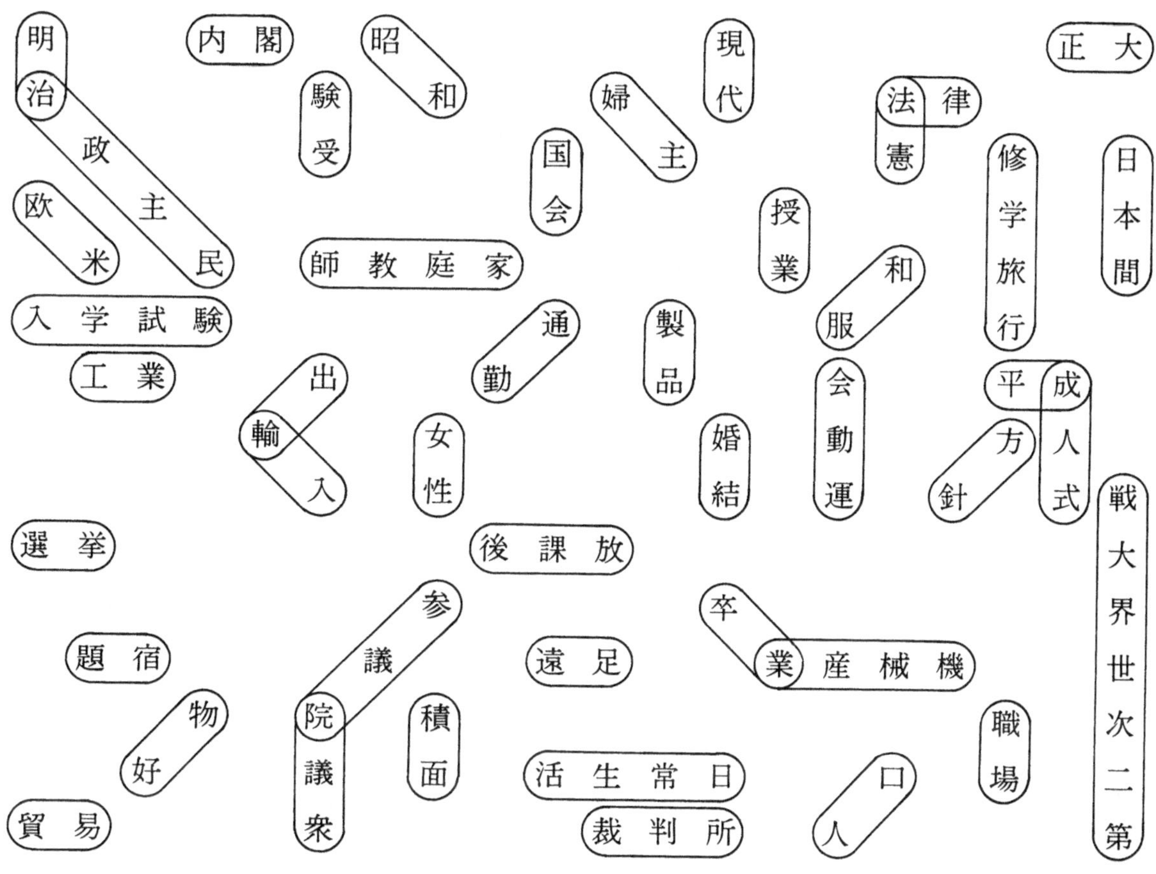

www.ingramcontent.com/pod-product-compliance
Lightning Source LLC
LaVergne TN
LVHW061251100826
845148LV00008B/1090

* 9 7 8 0 8 2 4 8 1 2 4 8 5 *